Interpreting
Sacred Ground

T0288193

Rhetoric, Culture, and Social Critique

Series Editor
John Louis Lucaites

Editorial Board
Barbara Biesecker
Carole Blair
Joshua Gunn
Robert Hariman
Debra Hawhee
Steven Mailloux
Raymie E. McKerrow
Toby Miller
Austin Sarat
Janet Staiger
Barbie Zelizer

Interpreting Sacred Ground

The Rhetoric of National Civil War Parks and Battlefields

J. CHRISTIAN SPIELVOGEL

THE UNIVERSITY OF ALABAMA PRESS
Tuscaloosa

The University of Alabama Press
Tuscaloosa, Alabama 35487-0380
uapress.ua.edu

Copyright © 2013 by the University of Alabama Press
All rights reserved.

Hardcover edition published 2013.
Paperback edition published 2021.
eBook edition published 2013.

Inquiries about reproducing material from this work should be addressed to the
University of Alabama Press.

Typeface: Bembo

Cover image: African Americans collecting bones of soldiers killed in battle,
photograph by John Reekie; courtesy Library of Congress
Cover design: Burt&Burt

Paperback ISBN: 978-0-8173-6018-4

A previous edition of this book has been cataloged by the Library of Congress.
ISBN: 978-0-8173-1775-1 (cloth)
E-ISBN: 978-0-8173-8631-3

Contents

Illustrations

Acknowledgments

I would like to express my heartfelt thanks to the many people who helped me over the course of my research on national Civil War parks and battlefields. I am grateful to Dan Waterman at The University of Alabama Press for his expert editorial advice and consultation, as well as series editor John Lucaites and the three anonymous reviewers for providing illuminating suggestions that expanded the clarity, focus, and overall strength of this book.

This book is interdisciplinary at its core and reflects insights from a variety of outstanding scholars and individuals across the fields of rhetoric and communication, Civil War history, and public history. In rhetoric and communication I thank Thomas W. Benson, gifted teacher, scholar, and master listener and synthesizer of information who exerted a tremendous influence on the project with the lightest touch; Stephen Browne, who opened my eyes to seeing the interpretive possibilities contained within public memory artifacts; and Michael Hogan, who guided me through the clutter of academic jargon and helped me say more while writing less. I want to acknowledge a group of fine Civil War historians who have tolerated a rhetorician's quest to uncover deeper meanings about the war and its place in public memory: Ed Ayers, Bill Blair, Bill Freehling, and Gary Gallagher. National Park Service rangers and historians graciously devoted their time and vast insights to this project. I am especially indebted to Scott Hartwig, John Hennessy, and Dwight Pitcaithley.

Hope College provided generous summer research support, and my colleagues in the Communication Department not only engaged me in constructive discussions about the manuscript, but their kindness and collegiality provided an inspiring context for writing and reflection.

I also wish to acknowledge my family. My children, Drew, Elena, and

Sean, provided many joyful detours to this book's completion. My parents, Jack and Diane Spielvogel, instilled in their children a thirst for learning. They are both eloquent speakers, writers, and teachers, and their professional talents are only eclipsed by their gifts as loving spouses and parents. Thanks, Mom and Dad, for setting the bar so high. And to my wife, Laurie: my inspiration and partner in life, love, and work.

Abbreviations

CHVC   Cold Harbor Visitor Center
GNMP   Gettysburg National Military Park
HFNHP Harpers Ferry National Historical Park
NPS   National Park Service

Interpreting
Sacred Ground

Introduction

Preservation or Interpretation? The National Park Service and Public Memory

This book examines how the National Park Service (NPS), through its interpretive history exhibits, invites the American public to interpret the legacy of their most divisive and destructive national event: the Civil War. A rhetorical analysis of the artifacts that the NPS uses to interpret the war at Civil War historical parks and battlefields—including field markers, orientation films, museum exhibits, and orientation brochures—reveals how the Park Service has constructed interpretations of the war and its enduring themes of reconciliation, racial conflict, emancipation, and the struggle for equality, the relationship between warfare and masculinity, and the morality of war.

The NPS has, since 1916, been the federal agency responsible for identifying, preserving, and interpreting public spaces deemed of historic, cultural, natural, and scenic national significance.[1] Currently the Park Service is committed to the dual objective of preserving and interpreting nearly four hundred public spaces of national importance to millions of visitors each year.[2] Not surprisingly, a federal agency with as much power and influence as the Park Service has been subjected to a fair amount of close scrutiny in a democratic society wary of excessive federal control over local, state, and private interests. However, the Park Service has traditionally been evaluated by scholars and the general public mostly on their ability as historical preservationists to restore those spaces with the appropriate measure of accuracy, authenticity, and discretion. Largely absent from bureaucratic, scholarly, and public discussion on the Park Service have been efforts to understand the Park Service's second objective: interpreting and creating meaning at these public spaces.[3]

Until the 1990s, the dominance of a preservationist orientation has been reflected in the Park Service's overall philosophy. The Park Service's main objective of preservation, in fact, defined their interpretive objectives. "First," explains former NPS assistant director Robert M. Utley when defining the management objectives of Park Service historical programs, "we were to care for 'historic resources' and guard them from whatever forces, natural or human (including our own managers), [that] endangered them. . . . Second, we were to 'interpret' these resources through museums, films, publications, lectures, tours, and other media, to give the visitor an understanding and appreciation of the resources and events being illustrated."[4] Preservation, as defined by Utley, is the material protection of historical sites from forces that would alter their original appearance, while "interpretation" amounts to verbal, written, or mediated "preservation" of the events that took place on those material landscapes. Therefore, interpretation has traditionally served the interests of historically accurate preservation and does not refer to the Park Service's own interpretations that function to actively create, and not just passively preserve, meanings and memories about the past.

A preservationist perspective also tends to prevail in academic scholarship about the Park Service outside the field of rhetorical studies, perhaps influenced by the Park Service's own preservationist agenda.[5] Those who evaluate the Park Service from a preservationist perspective tend either to assess the historical accuracy of the various structures and exhibits at a given park or to examine the conflicts between the Park Service and outside interest groups over whether or not landscapes of national importance should be preserved or used for economic gain.[6] Alternately, an interpretive perspective not defined by preservation objectives would involve understanding the rhetorical dimensions of NPS historical parks or the symbolic processes used in NPS interpretive exhibits to shape the meanings that park visitors are invited to construct about their collective past.[7]

A Rhetorical Analysis of National Park Service Interpretations of the Civil War

In this book, I conduct a close rhetorical analysis of how the Park Service interprets Gettysburg National Military Park (GNMP), Harpers Ferry National Historical Park (HFNHP), and Cold Harbor Visitor Center (CHVC), three of the most popular and important sites of Civil War memory. These three parks represent the past and present foci of Park Service interpretation of the Civil War. Spearheaded by the efforts of former Park Service chief historian Dwight T. Pitcaithley in the mid-1990s, followed by a decree from Congress in the late 1990s, the Park Service began developing interpretive exhibits that identified slavery as the principal cause of the Civil War.[8] Harpers Ferry National Historical Park represents one of the NPS's first concerted efforts to place slavery at the war's epicenter.

While the public memory of the war refashioned at Harpers Ferry National Historical Park emphasized racial conflict as a primary cause of the war, the majority of other Park Service Civil War battlefields have tended to develop sensitive interpretations of battle that stressed regional harmony and reconciliation between whites. For example, as early as the 1890s, the War Department used Civil War battlefields such as Gettysburg to both narrate the military history of battle and commemorate its white heroes. The contradiction between national integration and interracial segregation proves to be especially vexing at Gettysburg. In chapter 1 I tease apart this contradiction as I analyze how the Park Service interprets Abraham Lincoln's Gettysburg Address, which has been appropriated since its delivery by groups supportive of white reconciliation and African American emancipation and equality. Does the Park Service use the address, as various black activist groups did in the 1960s, to emphasize Lincoln's desire for a new postwar national identity based on the proposition that "all men are created equal," or does it select fragments from the message to commemorate the sacrifices of white soldiers from both sides who fought at Gettysburg?

I devote the second chapter of this study to an analysis of the Park Service's interpretation of John Brown's raid at Harpers Ferry and discuss how, if at all, exhibits developed in the 1990s in response to new calls to place slavery at the center of the war's meaning and memory alter the site's overall meaning and perhaps foreshadow a broader debunking of dominant Civil War public memory. I argue that the Park Service appropriates an "emancipationist memory" at Harpers Ferry National Historical Park to link John Brown's slave rebellion to a larger national narrative of twentieth-century racial progress and conclude that this interpretation, while positive, leaves visitors with the impression that racial inequality is a thing of the past.

Public memories of the Civil War are most commonly transmitted through battle narratives. What particular forms of memory are created through the Park Service's interpretation of battle? I have chosen to analyze the Park Service's interpretation of the battle of Gettysburg because its legendary place in Civil War history and memory is unchallenged by any other battle or event of the war. The battle, commonly recognized as "the beginning of the end" of the war, is where narratives of the conclusion of the war linger, locating the deeper meanings of the war's causes and legacies in Gettysburg's dramatic pathos. National white reconciliation has been dramatized through the twenty-five-, fifty-, and seventy-five-year veterans' reunions that took place at Gettysburg. These reunions, captured in photos of former enemies shaking hands over the spot where the Confederates reached their "High Water Mark," helped provide the country with its reunification iconography. Gettysburg, like the majority of other Park Service battlefields, is devoted to telling the military history of battle, but it stands apart as Gettysburg alone bears much of the war's commemorative weight.

I argue in chapters 3 and 4 that "white reconciliationist" memory informs the Park Service's characterization of combat violence at Gettysburg National Military Park. In chapter 3, I examine the interrelationship between dominant constructions of nineteenth-century prewar masculinity and late nineteenth-century national reconciliationist rhetoric that attempted to restore, to its cultural hegemony, a form of heroic masculinity challenged by the war's devastation. It was widely believed at the beginning of the war that victory would be assured for those who exhibited calm resolve, steadfast faith, and gentlemanly conduct in battle. This version of masculinity, which portrayed war as a moral activity that was an important, even necessary, rite of passage into manhood, was brutally undermined toward the end of the war by the repeated failure of unflinching frontal assaults, dishonorable fighting tactics, and the terrifying and depersonalized reality of trench warfare. I contend in chapter 4 that white reconciliationist memory functions rhetorically, through the physical landscape and medium of photography, to restore the ideology of heroic white masculinity to its prewar hegemony at GNMP, thereby marginalizing more savage interpretations of the war and upholding war as a morally desirable activity in the process.

How are Civil War commemorative traditions, I ask in chapter 5, used to interpret the final stages of a hard and destructive war in 1864–65? Using Cold Harbor Visitor Center as a site that typifies the war's final two savage years, I contend that reconciliationist and emancipationist public memories fail to achieve interpretive dominance at CHVC, thereby yielding to more savage interpretations of the battle that mark the landscape as a fixed, static place of struggle and death. As a result, the rhetorical form of CHVC does not follow the battle's chronological progression as it does at sites like Gettysburg but instead follows a structure of movement, stagnation, and death. Ironically, an inability to preserve the expansive battlefield creates an opening for more interpretive possibilities at Cold Harbor that would make it unique as compared to other fully preserved battlefields, producing what I argue is a harrowing and somber visitor experience.

The conclusion of this book summarizes the case for including the National Park Service as an important voice of twentieth- and twenty-first-century Civil War public memorializing and addresses several important questions about the future of interpretation at national Civil War military battlefields and parks. Overall, the three battlefields and historical parks examined in this book reflect the many themes and ideals that have been the source of intense cultural struggle for interpretive dominance of the war's legacy and memory. By attending closely to how these sites represent the past, I illustrate how the Park Service's interpretations of the war have contributed to and continue to shape the broader cultural struggle for interpretive dominance of the war's legacy.

Many of the themes and critiques in this book will be familiar to scholars and Park Service personnel attuned in recent years to how race and memory have impacted interpretation of the Civil War's meaning and legacy. According to Scott Hartwig, chief historian at GNMP, Civil War battlefields became a jumping-off point for larger questions for NPS chief historian Dwight Pitcaithley in the mid-1990s, and while "many line rangers took their jobs so they could interpret just the battle, they were being asked [by Pitcaithley] to tell a larger story."[9] That story, for John Hennessy, chief historian at Fredericksburg and Spotsylvania National Military Park, involves delicately balancing veneration for the soldiers who fought in the war and the generals who led them with historically accurate exhibits that identify slavery as the war's principal cause and black freedom as its most significant outcome. "We need to learn that when a government aligns itself with oppression," argues Hennessy when talking about slavery, "then bad things happen, and whole communities are destroyed by the experience of war."[10]

While those directly involved in interpreting national battlefields and parks are now sensitive to the repressive qualities of the reconciliationist commemorative tradition, an in-depth rhetorical analysis of these sites can illuminate a wider range of symbolic dimensions, including the ways in which military strategy narratives repress the centrality of the war's violence, the characteristic tendencies of NPS interpretation during different time periods, and the visual rhetoric of preserved landscapes. I invite Park Service personnel, scholars, park visitors, and students to imagine these landscapes as I do—not only as the source of important historical details and facts but as the site of variable rival public memories that struggle to gain interpretive dominance over the past.

The Civil War remains an epochal event in U.S. history. Historian Alice Fahs argues, "just as the Civil War was a defining event in our national history, so too have memories of the Civil War helped define membership in the nation."[11] Fahs indicates that the Civil War, a central turning point in the country's history, still stands as a benchmark for the construction of America's national identity. The war's legacy is also apparent on the country's physical landscape, as thousands of plaques, field markers, and memorials record and honor the actions of Union and Confederate soldiers and generals during the war.[12] Approximately twenty Civil War battlefields have been interpreted by the NPS, while another thirty historic parks and monuments relate to the Civil War era. In fact, the NPS devotes more sites to interpreting the Civil War than to the American Revolution, World Wars I and II, and Vietnam combined. If the control over public space has a powerful influence over memory, then the Park Service's ownership of nearly fifty public spaces relating to the war would appear to exert a significant influence on Civil War memory.

But why exactly are memories of such a distant war so important today? In part, the answers to many important questions about public policy and national identity following the war hinged on how the war and its legacy would be interpreted.[13] By war's end, many questions about the country's future were open to debate, at least as seen in retrospect. Implicit in these debates, for example, were questions about what ideas and values would serve as the common ground for a possible renewed nationalism. Whose interests would be served by reconciliation? Would the country follow emancipation by dedicating itself to "a new birth of freedom" for all Americans, or would freedom and citizenship continue to be restricted along racial lines? Would the country reject the war's shocking and unprecedented levels of death as a tragic and needless loss of human life, or would the dead be recast as heroes who embodied the masculine ideal, effectively reinvigorating patriotism based on martial heroism?

Explanations of the war's meaning and memory would influence not just public policy in the period of Reconstruction following the war, however. The needs and concerns of the present always constrain how the past is interpreted. Therefore, memories of the conflict that ended slavery, began mass warfare, and altered the boundaries of cultural identity serve as an ideal lens through which to understand judgments of race, war, masculinity, power, and national identity in all of the decades since the war.[14] Reciprocally, dominant memories of the Civil War shape perceptions of race, war, masculinity, power, and national identity for all generations since the war.[15] For example, it might seem normal or natural for us today to understand the Civil War as a battle between two regions of soldiers who fought with equal valor and courage for what they believed in, regardless of their causes. However, this understanding of the war reflects what Edward Linenthal calls an "ideology of reconciliation." Developed in the late nineteenth century, this dominant national memory of the war made reunification between northern and southern whites possible by emphasizing white martial heroism to the exclusion of blacks and questions of racial equality.[16] The extent to which the ideology of reconciliation seems natural today suggests that the war's dominant memory has helped construct an exclusionary national identity that has been "preserved" since the late nineteenth century.

Scholarship on public memory of the Civil War has not directly identified and assessed the Park Service's key role as an arbiter of twentieth-century Civil War memory. In fact, with some important exceptions, the majority of studies of Civil War memorializing focus on the period between the end of the Civil War and the beginning of World War I.[17] One reason for this omission has been the appearance of a relatively unified, consensual, and therefore static national memory of the war influenced by the period of national reconciliation and the demand for "realist" representations of the war in the late 1880s and 1890s.[18] Collectively, these factors helped make twentieth-century Civil War memorializing appear less symbolic and more literal or mimetic in its structure, thus rendering interpretive debates of the war's meaning less necessary and explicit. By including the Park Service as an important arbiter of Civil War memory, this study fills an important gap in the literature on the Civil War in public memory and can help assess the Park Service's role in reflecting and/or popularizing dominant national memories of the Civil War.

So that readers might fully grasp my perspective on the Park Service's role in constructing Civil War memory, I will outline the theoretical, historical, and methodological framework that informs my approach. First, I begin by defining public memory and explaining the importance of consensual understandings of the past in shaping the course of a community's present and future, particularly during periods of cultural transition such as the Civil War. Second, I demonstrate that repressive dominant memories can slow important social and political changes, making it necessary to understand public memory as an argumentative struggle between rival versions of the past so that those marginalized memories can be used to productively critique the limitations of a dominant public memory. Third, I review other scholarship that, taken together, provides a brief history of how different groups in the late nineteenth century used public space in an attempt to gain interpretive dominance of the war's legacy. Finally, I argue for the inclusion of the Park Service as a central voice in twentieth- and twenty-first-century interpretations of the war's meaning and legacy, and illustrate how a preservationist orientation has historically constrained awareness of the Park Service's role in interpreting the war's legacy.

Public Memory

John Bodnar defines public memory as "a body of beliefs and ideas about the past that help a public or society understand both its past, present, and by implication, its future."[19] Bodnar's definition underscores the importance of public memory as a foundation for collective judgment and action. In his study on Jewish Holocaust memorials, James Young argues that scholars of public memory should not ask whether a given act of memorializing reflects past history accurately or fashionably but should discover how a text about the past "suggests itself as a basis for political and social action."[20] For example, Stephen Browne's study of Daniel Webster's 1820 Plymouth Rock Oration illustrates how Webster attempts to stabilize his audience's adherence to official values by linking them to certain Whig notions of tradition. Control over how past events should be interpreted serves as a powerful justification for maintaining attitudes and directing action.

The social and political stakes for control over public memory can indeed be very significant, especially during periods of social and political transition whereby memories of the past are used to gain a sense of direction and control over the uncertain present and future. This tendency toward cultural redefinition and transformation is especially evident in the aftermath of war, which tends to bring about more revolutionary social and political changes. In the words of historian Michael Sherry, war has been the "paradigm in which Americans defined themselves, pursued change, or resisted it."[21] This theme is echoed by Michael Kammen, who argues in his study of the history of American tradition: "Wars have played a fundamental role in stimulating, defining, justifying, periodizing, and eventually filtering American memories and traditions."[22] We can add to Sherry and Kammen's comments that it is not just the experience of war itself that influences social and political change, but it is the interpretations of American war experiences that shape the course of the country's attitudes and beliefs.[23] The cultural struggle over how to interpret the past as a way to guide future social and political action becomes especially intense during periods of cultural transition.

Because the stakes for control over public memory can be so significant, it would seem logical that many groups would compete for interpretive dominance of the past. In fact, assuming that a singular "public memory" exists ignores the process of rhetorical struggle that enables one interpretation of the past to gain dominance over rival interpretations in the first place. David W. Blight, for example, defines public memory as "the study of cultural struggle, of contested truths, interpretations, moments, events, epochs, rituals, or even texts in history that thresh out rival versions of the past which are in turn put to the service of the present."[24] Moreover, overlooking the simultaneous existence of multiple public memories can make dominant public memories such as the ideology of reconciliation mentioned earlier appear unified and consensual. And without the explicit contest over memory, a community is less likely to critically engage the past, and, therefore, a stable sense of identity and consensus is likely to be maintained.[25]

If society were egalitarian, then perhaps we could rely on stable public memories and avoid the need to arouse debates over how to interpret the past. However, as David Blight, Kirk Savage, and Edward Linenthal have observed, one of the consequences of the reconciliation ideology was the cessation of movements toward broader equality along racial and class lines. One way to invigorate public memory debates is to resurrect marginalized interpretations of the war's legacy in order to see the dominant public memory as socially constructed, contested, and variable.

Public Memory of the Civil War:
Contested Nineteenth-Century Interpretations

The struggle for interpretive dominance of Civil War memory was largely rhetorical. As David Blight argues, control over public memory of the war "was the prize in a struggle between rival versions of the past, a question of will, of power, of persuasion. The historical memory of any transforming or controversial event emerges from cultural and political competition, from the choice to confront the past and to debate and manipulate its meaning."[26]

As Blight and others argue, however, the meanings associated with the war's legacy were by no means inevitable as the nation faced the era of Reconstruction. Kirk Savage argues that emancipation challenged the nation to reimagine the meaning of freedom, and he analyzes the use of public space in the nineteenth century as a way to understand the possibilities of a new interracial order. "What," Savage asks, "would freedom mean in a society who uses racial difference to justify slavery? Could race be reimagined?"[27] Savage argues that during the period of Reconstruction the answer to these questions varied significantly across regional boundaries, although certain similarities that transcended Northern and Southern war memorializing helped facilitate reconciliation at a terrible cost.

The Confederate capital of Richmond served as the center of Southern Lost Cause memorializing and was reflected in the key figure of Robert E. Lee. According to Savage, Lee represented a depoliticized, military hero figure that enabled the Lost Cause to "become a story of glorious military achievement rather than a struggle to secure a slaveholding nation." This image of Lee as a leader of soldiers rather than policy provided Southerners with a hero in their own postwar image that "helped reestablish old lines of racial sympathy."[28]

Because physical beauty has been linked with intellect and culture, and sculpture itself has traditionally been concerned with idealized human forms, Savage argues that Northern monuments, while recognizing emancipation, did so not through a liberation of the black body but through the politicized image of Abraham Lincoln. The figures of Lee and Lincoln, then, functioned to metonymize Civil War memory in the South and the North, as each individual served as the vessel for regional attitudes toward the war, race, and cultural identity. Furthermore, each region created a hero in its own image during the last third of the nineteenth century that was not necessarily national in its appeal.

The use of public space to etch a region's memory of the war permanently on the landscape was the product of well-coordinated institutional and organizational efforts. Through monuments, histories, literature, and rituals, veterans' organizations were used to promote partisan histories of the war, especially in the South, where membership in organizations such as the United Daughters of the Confederacy and the Sons of Confederate Veterans consistently exceeded those of similar organizations in the North. Thomas Connelly and Barbara L. Bellow argue that an "inner" Lost Cause pervaded the South in the 1870s and early 1880s.[29] Veterans' organizations, inspired by the words of former Confederate leaders and generals such as Jefferson Davis and Jubal Early, argued that the South was never defeated in courage or spirit but simply was unable to match the Union's superior manpower and resources. Much like the public sculpture produced in the South during this period, Lost Cause rhetoric downplayed the deeper causes of Southern secession and instead focused on the battlefields of the war itself and the generals who honored or betrayed the Confederacy.

By the 1890s, argue Connelly and Bellows, the Lost Cause became more familiar as a national movement that projected the nostalgic image of a chivalrous and romantic Old South.[30] Literature played an important role in this shift. Especially influential were novels written by Southern women that promoted intersectional harmony through the de-

piction of a genteel South where slaves and slave owners alike lived together in relative tranquility. Although a more feminized image of the
South helped pave the way for intersectional reunion, by the late nineteenth century reunification became increasingly associated with what
Alice Fahs calls a "whites-only brotherhood" forged between Confederate and Union veterans. By the mid-1890s, argue Kurt Piehler and
Kirk Savage, this fraternity of arms began to show up in public space,
as a new type of monument dedicated to the ordinary white volunteer
soldier emerged in the North and South in remarkably similar ways. Ultimately, the catastrophe of mass warfare fueled the desire to pay tribute to the citizen soldier in public spaces across the country.[31] In both
North and South, the common soldier monument tended to portray a
lone white soldier who was neither engaged in combat nor showed any
visible signs of war's calamity.

While "traditions of racist thought entrenched in slavery acted as a
drag on [social] change" during the period of Reconstruction, Savage
argues that "mass warfare propelled public monuments into a new era of
militarism."[32] As Cruce Stark persuasively argues, "the acceptance of the
Southern soldier into the fraternity of arms was a necessary final distilla-
tion of the soldier into a distinct element of society. The line of separa-
tion ... was not now between North and South, but between those who
had tested their manhood in the fire of battle and those who had not."[33]

The "romance of reunion," as Nina Silber has called it, which was often typified by pictures of older Confederate and Union veterans shaking hands over the chasms of former lines of battle, might have appeared
transcendent if not for a few dissenting countermemories of the war's
legacy and meaning. Frederick Douglass's interpretation of the war's meaning and legacy, for example, reveals that the "whites-only brotherhood"
of the 1890s was achieved at the expense of black Americans. As Blight
argues, Douglass's attempts to sanctify Northern victory in the 1870s and
1880s were just as partisan as early Lost Cause efforts in the South, although instead of rationalizing defeat, Douglass insisted on the righteousness of Northern victory over a region that supported slavery.

Douglass, Blight contends, "seemed acutely aware that the postwar
era might ultimately be controlled by those who could best shape interpretations of the war itself."[34] Douglass used his awareness of the power
of historical memory to designate emancipation and black freedom as

the war's lasting legacy for shaping the country's future national purpose: "Douglass hoped that Union victory, black emancipation, and the Civil War amendments would be so deeply rooted in recent American experience, so central to any conception of national regeneration, so necessary to the postwar society that they would become sacred values, ritualized in memory."[35]

By the 1890s, however, Douglass's attempts to create an emancipationist commemorative tradition would be swept aside by the emotions of sentimental reunion. A dominant public memory of the war that triumphed in the manly valor of its common soldiers would emerge and find repeated expression in emotional veterans' reunions, patriotic speeches, and public sculpture honoring the common soldier. In short, while public Civil War memorializing did not contribute much to the acceleration of a new interracial order in the last third of the nineteenth century, the popularity of a "reconstructed" white masculinity helped produce a hero figure that transcended regional differences, glorified military heroism, and would serve as the foundation for national Civil War memorializing in the twentieth century.

Centralizing Civil War Memory in the Twentieth Century

The federal government first began taking steps to honor the common soldier through the creation of national cemeteries. At the peak of the reconciliation movement in 1890, Congress authorized the first two national military parks, Chickamauga and Chattanooga National Military Park and Antietam National Battlefield Park. By 1900, Shiloh, Gettysburg, and Vicksburg were also added to the list, and all five sites were administered by the War Department. By 1906, Congress had authorized an extensive system of permanent cemeteries for the war dead.[36] According to former NPS administrator Edwin C. Bearss, each military park was administered by a three-man commission that was given a mandate to mark troop positions, movements, and fighting on iron tablets to be placed in their appropriate locations on a given site of battle.

These sites, representing both the northern, southern, and western frontiers of the war, were themselves depoliticized, as the focus on Civil War battlefield memorials to common soldiers and generals enabled both the North and the South to minimize the political and social issues surrounding the conflict.[37] Kurt Piehler, in his study on American war memory, argues that this burdened the federal government with the task of eulogizing the war's dead, although "death and destruction were not ignored; they retained a heroic quality and were represented as serving a transcendent purpose."[38] In addition to serving as the meeting place for joint Union and Confederate reunions in the late 1890s and early 1900s, Congress mandated that the battlefields be used as a military training ground for U.S. Army officers to study military strategy and terrain.

In 1906, Congress passed the Act for Preservation of American Antiquities, which gave the federal government unprecedented control over the preservation of land.[39] When the General Land Office of the Department of the Interior was renamed the National Park Service in 1916, its director, Stephen T. Mather, vowed to prioritize the preservation of natural splendor at the over twenty western parks and monuments. At least initially, the act helped facilitate the preservation of natural spaces that reflected what Bodnar calls "scenic nationalism."[40]

Natural Parks: The National Park Service and the Origins of a Preservationist Perspective

Prior to assuming administrative control over all federally owned national parks, battlefields, cemeteries, and monuments in 1933, the NPS had been responsible for preserving federally owned natural and archaeological landscapes. The NPS began to emphasize the preservation of the nation's historical past in the mid-1930s, which quickly led to the establishment of a comprehensive interpretive history program that would be used to explain those preserved historic spaces. In the process, the NPS developed a set of criteria for adding new spaces to the park system. By 1937, a site was likely to be preserved and interpreted if it was associated with the major themes of American history, contained strong ties to famous Americans, or reflected dramatic episodes of American history.[41]

Eventually the NPS's control over public space would lead it to play an important role in interpreting not only the Civil War but also the country's past from a national perspective. Yet despite its changing role as a custodian of America's historical memory, the ubiquity of a preservationist orientation would continue to overshadow the Park Service's role in actively constructing national memory. This preservationist perspective has constrained the nature and scope of potentially important "interpretation debates" that could challenge the limitations of dominant national memories. Instead, a series of "preservation debates," while important, reveal that the public has consistently supported Park Service initiatives, helping make it one of the most popular federal agencies in the country. A review of those debates illustrates how a preservationist orientation has historically obscured awareness of the Park Service's role in interpreting the Civil War and American history generally.

Debates over Natural and Historic Preservation: An Overview

Scholarship on the NPS and preservation has chronicled the often bitter debates between preservationists and pro-growth advocates over proposals for commercial, industrial, or residential development on or near Park Service lands. Time and again these debates have created particular alliances and antagonisms: the landowning public, historians, and environmentalists have tended to respond favorably to the Park Service's call for preserving the country's heritage, while local and state politicians, developers, and other business interests line up on the side of pro-growth because it will presumably expand the tax base. The polarized nature of these debates often forces the public to make a choice between private and public (for example, federal government) control over its most cherished material landscapes. Given the usually crass commercialization of history by economically motivated private interests, it appears obvious why the Park Service would be considered a more respectable national curator.

The interests and issues in debates over the preservation of natural parks are different in several ways from debates over historical parks, although both would appear to contain these differences within the tension between "preservation" and "development" or "material growth." On the one hand, debates concerning preservation of the Park Service's natural parks tend to revolve around environmental issues and the proper use of natural resources. On the other hand, disputes about the commercial or residential development of historic lands controlled by the Park Service—especially battlefields—tend to involve questions about when, if it all, it is acceptable to develop or encroach on "sacred ground."

Natural Preservation Debates

Many scholars justify their endorsement of the Park Service by contrasting the embarrassing defacement of Niagara Falls by private commercial interests with the more successful federal effort to establish and preserve Yellowstone National Park in 1872. For these authors, the late 1800s rather than the 1930s were pivotal in explaining the Park Service's influence. William C. Everhart's comments on Niagara Falls are typical:

> It was the misfortune that blighted Niagra Falls, at one time the most famous and popular tourist attraction in the United States, that convinced a good many people the nation should take steps when one of its scenic marvels was being desecrated. Soon after 1800 the land around the falls began to slip into the hands of tourist promoters. Eventually the rim was almost filled with blocks of dreary and vulgar shops and catchpenny booths. Travelers were hustled and harassed and fleeced. By 1860 there was no point on the U.S. side from which the falls could be seen without paying some sharpie a fee. The commercialization and defacement of Niagra Falls became the country's first environmental disgrace.[42]

The interpretive framework for Everhart's study is clearly established here, and his explanation of the failure to properly preserve Niagara Falls is used as a justification for federal control of landscapes. Quite simply, the Park Service emerged as a more environmentally conscious and tasteful alternative to the short-sighted, profit-driven motives of commercial "tourist promoters."

Alfred Runte, in his book *National Parks: The American Experience,* traces the numerous debates between advocates of environmental preservation and material progress that erupted in the nineteenth and twentieth centuries. These debates often arose when the Park Service began to take steps to establish a new national park, and manufacturers would insist that the NPS restrict park acreage to areas that contained the fewest natural resources available for exploitation. The Park Service appeared more often than not to side with the conservationists in these debates, but Runte argues that, in reality, the Park Service did not want to alienate the interests of material progress and therefore often chose to preserve scenic vistas that contained little economic value.

The selection of great natural wonders such as Yellowstone National Park and the Grand Canyon National Monument as national parks was seen by many as a proud reflection of the country's distinctive landscape.

During the late 1800s and early 1900s, Runte argues, many elites in the United States were searching for proof of national greatness and tradition. For many journalists, artists, historians, and politicians, the discovery of the frontier provided the best evidence of national distinctiveness, and so the region's mountains and canyons were often favorably compared to the natural landscapes of Europe. The preservation of scenic landscapes, then, played an integral role in the development of a national tradition and identity that were described as superior to Europe's own natural wonders.

It is important to note that the Park Service's approach to the protection of historic sites emerged from their years of experience with preserving scenic landscapes. Moreover, the public itself has been invited to experience and evaluate the Park Service's representation of history based on a tacit understanding of the "park" concept. Hence, many NPS-owned historic sites are today named "National Historic Parks" and contain the natural wonders people come to expect with the outdoor recreational opportunities (for example, hiking and photography) and scenic vistas provided by the Park Service. It should come as no surprise, then, that the Park Service's development of a comprehensive interpretive history program would be greatly influenced by the objectives that informed the preservation of natural spaces deemed worthy of national significance.

Historical Parks: The National Park Service and the Origins of Historical Interpretation

The 1906 Act for Preservation of American Antiquities was intended to lead to the federal preservation of scenic natural landscapes. But the law was ambiguous enough to accommodate changing federal priorities over time, which made it possible for the president and Congress to preserve the country's historical past as well.[43]

Former NPS director Horace Albright was determined to expand the scope and credibility of the NPS by first gaining centralized control over all federal parks, cemeteries, battlefields, and monuments and then increase visitation to these sites by adding a concern for historical interpretation and education to an otherwise aesthetic experience. His view was shared by Verne Chatelain, who was hired in 1931 as the first NPS historian and put in charge of establishing a rationale for a systematic presentation of America's historical past. By 1934 Chatelain had rejected the Park Service's administration over what he perceived to be historical sites that represented only random episodes of American history.[44] His solution was to develop a comprehensive approach to interpreting the country's past, thereby contextualizing those random episodes of American history within a larger cultural narrative that stressed national loyalty and progress.

In Chatelain's words, national areas were to be "carefully chosen upon the basis of important phases of American history" that would reflect "an adequate story of American progress from the earliest beginnings of human existence down to comparatively recent times."[45] According to Rothman, "the larger 'patterns of history' were what Chatelain sought, and rather than search for the story of each battlefield and house, Chatelain advocated exploring the larger questions and subsequently relating individual areas to broad themes."[46] By 1935, the Park Service had become the first federal agency in the United States responsible for promoting a coherent narrative about the country's historical, archaeological, and aesthetic past.

The development of a coherent interpretive history program—and by implication the attempt to construct a more stable and clearly recognizable national purpose and identity—could only be maintained through a large but efficient federal bureaucratic system. Chatelain's push for developing interpretive programs that referenced an orderly and coherent past resulted in the development of guidelines for the designation of site importance. To prevent every small-town organization from making a claim for historical significance, Chatelain successfully argued that the Park Service would recognize only sites that offered an outline of the major themes of American history. In addition, the sites had to be connected to the lives of famous Americans and were required to be located where dramatic episodes in American history had taken place.[47] By early 1937, Chatelain's proposal had become the backbone of NPS interpretive history programs at its seventy-seven historical sites.

Historic Battlefield Preservation Debates

Natural and historic national parks have typically been subjected to the same types of assessment and evaluation. Although environmental issues play an important role in debates over historic preservation, the relative proximity of historic sites to populated regions and developable land inspires conflicts over the appropriateness of commercial and residential development on historic lands of national importance. Battlefield preservation produces its own set of unique constraints over the seemingly incompatible goals of preservation and growth. As explained by scholars and activists, battlefield preservation controversies raise serious issues about whether or not historical landscapes should be preserved, who gets to preserve them, and how their preservation or commercial annexation will affect a community's economic future.

Similar to the justification of "scenic nationalism" used to promote and protect the country's western parks in the nineteenth century, battlefield preservation scholars argue that Civil War battlefields in particular should be preserved because they provide a link to understanding the foundations of a new national consciousness. They argue that "freezing" the landscape to its Civil War–era appearance provides scholars and the general public with an authentic re-creation of space that enables visitors to understand the tremendous sacrifices soldiers made to support their ideals.[48] Zenzen, for example, argues that "[c]ultural values are passed, and lessons are learned" when walking through the battlefields, and "[f]rom this experience, many Americans have come to view the battlegrounds as 'sacred ground,' hallowed by the sacrifices of the soldiers who gave their lives in support of their ideals."[49]

However, these descriptions of the war's moral significance that are used as justifications for preservation would appear to depend on subjective interpretations of the war's meaning rather than on historically accurate preservation values. By stressing preservation, some scholars fail to recognize that their patriotic veneration reflects an ideology of reconciliation forged through the veterans' reunions in the late 1880s and early 1890s. Therefore, the deeper cultural values cited by each author as justification for preservation are actually the product of values "frozen" from the late 1880s and early 1890s and in no way reflected popular sentiment "as it was" during the 1860s.

An "Interpretive (R)evolution"

While preservation tends to shape the meaning of interpretation in battlefield preservation scholarship, recent changes in NPS policies toward interpretation combined with a congressional mandate to include slavery as the principal cause of the war at NPS battlefield sites have opened the door to a reconsidered approach to historic interpretation. Concerned that historic parks presented "one-dimensional" histories of preserved structures and landscapes that were isolated from respected academic scholarship and more challenging forms of historical inquiry, NPS director Roger G. Kennedy (1993–97), chief historian Dwight Pitcaithley (1995–2005), and chief of interpretation Corky Mayo (1993–2009) dramatically enhanced the scope and credibility of NPS interpretive programs. Kennedy, the first trained historian to serve as director of the Park Service, initiated cooperative agreements between the agency and the Organization of American Historians; Pitcaithley developed a philosophy of education that emphasized the critical importance of historical literacy to a thriving democracy and strengthened the credibility of the NPS's interpretive programs by incorporating recognized scholarship into its interpretive programs; and Mayo created an "Interpretive Revolution" by developing rigorous training standards that placed a greater emphasis on interpretive content.[50]

One of the most visible outcomes of the Park Service's new interpretive focus was a group of battlefield superintendents' decision to situate Civil War battlefield narratives within a broader historical context that emphasized slavery as the principal cause of the war. This 1998 initiative was followed in 2000 by an Interior Department funding bill sponsored by Representative Jesse Jackson Jr. that required the Park Service to stress "the unique role that the institution of slavery played in causing the Civil War and its role, if any, in individual battle sites."[51]

Jackson's edict was aimed at getting the Park Service to stop allowing the minutiae of military strategy to prevent it from interpreting slavery as a primary cause of the war (and black freedom as one of its primary outcomes). New artifacts at places like Gettysburg and Corinth, Mississippi, respond directly to Jackson's challenge, appropriating an emancipationist memory of the war that challenges visitors to think critically about the war's causes and legacy. A sign that greets visitors entering the exhibit gallery at Gettysburg's new Museum and Visitor Center, for example, states: "The Civil War was fought over three issues—survival of the Union, the fate of slavery and . . . what it means to be an American. The war resolved the first two issues. The nation struggles with the third to this day."

Historians and memory scholars have also helped spur the changes in interpretation. According to Scott Hartwig, noted Civil War historian Eric Foner wrote an influential letter to the NPS urging the agency to shift Gettysburg's narrative from the theme of "celebrating Confederate courage" to "the far more inclusive theme of 'a new birth of freedom'" for the four million slaves emancipated during the war. A team of historians led by Nina Silber, David Blight, and James McPherson then recommended after a trip to Gettysburg that the military park shift its story to a broader narrative, which was received positively by NPS historians, as long as it satisfied the conditions of historical accuracy and integrity.[52]

Wresting interpretation loose from the strictures of preservationist objectives has the potential to produce new debates—for example, about whether or not the annexation of an entire battlefield is always necessary in order to facilitate reflection about abstract national values. The abstract values of tragedy, sacrifice, and heroism, for example, could be symbolically represented on some battlefields through one particular monument or the interpretation of one decisive point of engagement. While the preservation of an entire battlefield has tremendous public and scholarly educational value, partial holdings of battlefields do not have to be thought of as somehow preventing "complete" preservation and interpretation. Instead, partial holdings could sometimes be conceived of as opportunities to change and even broaden the context for interpreting the events that unfolded on those landscapes, enabling the Park Service to balance their tactical narratives with broader narratives about the war's causes and enduring legacy.

A rhetorical analysis of the deeper meanings contained within NPS historic parks and battlefields not only can provide timely feedback to an agency with a renewed commitment to expanding its view of historic interpretation but can illuminate the Park Service's unique commemorative voice in influencing ongoing public memory debates about the war's deeper meanings and legacies.

I
Race and Memory

1

"We Are Met on a Great Battle-Field"

Race, Memory, and the Gettysburg Address

Gettysburg, a pivotal symbol of Civil War memory, is best known for two events: the battle itself, fought July 1–3, 1863, and Abraham Lincoln's Gettysburg Address, delivered at the Gettysburg National Cemetery dedication a little over four months after the battle. Although Civil War enthusiasts still revel in the specific decisions made by men named Bragg, Rosecrans, and Burnside at places such as Chickamauga, Stones River, and Spotsylvania, the battle of Gettysburg and Lincoln's address have increasingly served to condense fading public memories of a long and bitter war fought over 150 years ago.

Abraham Lincoln's Gettysburg Address is widely recognized as one of the most eloquent and masterful orations in American history, yet its meaning remains seemingly transparent.[1] Its universality, for example, was the rationale for its inclusion in New York City's first commemoration of the terrorist attacks of September 11, 2001, an event carefully managed to avoid any semblance of local or national party politics.[2] The speech's sweeping ambiguity, brevity, and eloquence, however, have actually enhanced its utility as a polysemic text appropriated to suit a variety of competing political and ideological interests since its delivery. By tracing the speech's history in public memory, for example, Barry Schwartz finds that the address has been appropriated to serve the often contradictory interests of those who supported Reconstruction, post–Civil War regional reconciliation between whites, Progressive reform, World Wars I and II, and the civil rights movement of the 1960s.[3]

Despite its continued influence and history of complex appropriation and reception, rhetorical scholars have limited their scholarship on the address to studies of its original production, internal rhetorical dynamics, and immediate reception.[4] For example, scholars have attributed the speech's sacred qualities to its internal eloquence and organic structure, citing a universal narrative of redemption and salvation as a formal source of its appeal. These studies, while fruitful for their explication of the speech's aesthetics, unwittingly contribute to the perception that the Gettysburg Address has conveyed, through its stylistic artistry, unchanging, transcendent meanings since its delivery in November 1863.[5]

This chapter attempts to expand our understanding of the address by examining the ongoing rhetorical struggle to gain interpretive dominance over its meaning and public memory.[6] Conflicting interpretations of the address are perhaps most salient in white and African American public memories of the Civil War, whereby select fragments from Lincoln's address have consistently been used as warrants to support either a harmonious vision of postwar regional reconciliation between whites or a commitment to postwar racial justice and equality.

Developed in the late nineteenth century, the dominant national "reconciliationist" memory of the war accelerated reunification between northern and southern whites by emphasizing white martial heroism to the exclusion of blacks and questions of racial equality.[7] Bitter partisan memories of the Civil War gave way during this period to a dominant interpretation of the battlefield—this commemorative tradition's symbolic center—as a site of regional healing and transcendence. Dramatized in emotional veterans' reunions, patriotic speeches, public sculpture honoring the common soldier, and inscrutably detailed battle narratives, reconciliationist memory invited audiences to ignore or forget race-related causes and consequences of the war by commemorating the equal valor and heroism exhibited by white Union and Confederate soldiers in battle.[8] Lincoln, too, emerged during this time as Savior of the Union, and the *epainesis* of his address (lines 6–15) was often used to support the reconciliationists' claim that Lincoln eulogized the manly courage and sacrifice of white Northern and Southern common soldiers alike in his speech.[9]

There were those, of course, who did not stand to benefit from what at the turn of the twentieth century had become a reinvigorated ethnic nationalism constructed through the nostalgic pathos of depoliticized battlefield memory. White reconciliation went hand in hand with racial discrimination, as evidenced most vividly by Jim Crow laws, the soaring popularity of the Ku Klux Klan, and films such as D. W. Griffith's *Birth of a Nation*. Try as they might, African Americans could not popularize a memory of the war as Northern triumph over slavery and racism until later in the twentieth century.

Civil War battlefields and the ideology of white reconciliation—their lockstep had forced its critics to find other story lines from outside the battlefield to create politicized memories of the war's causes, consequences, and future legacy. Lincoln's Gettysburg Address, despite its battlefield location, would come to serve as one of these alternative story lines. Appropriated regularly by advocates of what David Blight calls "emancipationist memory," fragments from the speech were used as evidence that Lincoln envisioned a post–Civil War United States dedicated to the proposition "that all men are created equal."[10]

This chapter examines how the National Park Service appropriates these public memories of the war to commemorate the Gettysburg Address at Gettysburg National Military Park (GNMP).[11] The research for this chapter was undertaken prior to the unveiling of the 139,000-square-foot Museum and Visitor Center complex in April 2008. While the end of this chapter is devoted to an analysis of the new visitor center and its use of emancipationist memory, a majority of the artifacts examined in the rest of the chapter have been a permanent fixture on the GNMP battlefield and cemetery landscape for decades, while those that have been removed can help reveal the Park Service's shifting interpretive focus.

GNMP, a six-thousand-acre historical park visited by nearly two million people a year, is administered by the Park Service for the purpose of preserving and interpreting land where the battle of Gettysburg was fought and Lincoln delivered his famous eulogy. A close analysis of the Park Service's interpretation of the address reveals how commemorative practices permeate the predominantly historical discourse at the site and thereby constitute a public memory of Lincoln's speech. How, I ask, does the Park Service use the reconciliationist and emancipationist commemorative traditions to interpret the address? Do they use the address, as various black activist groups did in the 1960s, to emphasize Lincoln's desire that "all men are created equal," or do park exhibits display fragments from the message to commemorate the sacrifices of white soldiers from both sides who fought at Gettysburg? Or does the NPS invite a polysemic reading of the address by creating a space for both interpretations to coexist?

Overall, I contend that the Park Service uses Lincoln's address as an eloquent expression of white regional reconciliation. Dedicated primarily to interpreting the battle of Gettysburg, interpretive exhibits at GNMP interweave historical detail and reunionist sentiment to perpetuate the public memory of white reconciliation so typical of battlefield representation. This mixture of history and commemoration functions rhetorically to make the ideology of white reconciliation seem like a historical, and therefore objective, chronicle of the battle. Under the weight of what is predominantly a battle narrative, the lines (6–15) from Lincoln's address that refer to the temporal present and the spatial context of the cemetery are used in Park Service exhibits to commemorate the equal valor and heroism of white Union and Confederate soldiers who fought at Gettysburg. I conclude the chapter by suggesting that the Park Service's use of emancipationist memory in its new Museum and Visitor Center has helped to make GNMP a site of contested public memory, which likely will generate invaluable "interpretation debates" in the decades to follow.

Gettysburg Address Interpretation: Gettysburg National Military Park Visitor Center

Gettysburg National Military Park, with its more than six thousand acres of land, can be a bit overwhelming without an initial trip to the visitor center. In addition to providing visitors with information and maps of the park, the visitor center contains interpretive materials that condense the park's overall interpretive focus. Rhetorically, the visitor center helps provide the interpretive framework that will shape visitors' initial perceptions of the site.

Although the battle of Gettysburg takes up the vast majority of park space and interpretation, the address's symbolic importance to overall NPS Gettysburg interpretation becomes apparent when walking up to the main information and check-in counter at the visitor center. Three large framed collages, complete with photographs of the park and selected quotations from Lincoln's address, are logically arranged from left to right on the wall behind the main desk and greet tourists as they begin their tour of the battlefield and cemetery. The first collage features a line from Lincoln's speech ("We are met on a great battle-field") that seems to

Figure 1.1. Handshake over the stone wall, Gettysburg seventy-fifth anniversary reunion. (Photograph courtesy of National Park Service.)

underscore the site's historic significance and includes an iconic photograph of two former adversaries shaking hands over the stone wall near the Angle during the seventy-fifth anniversary of Gettysburg reunion.

The fragment from Lincoln's address, if read independently of the accompanying photograph, lacks a commemorative context. If anything, reading the fragment without the photographs would function to contextualize the visitor within his or her immediate surroundings, making it seem as if Lincoln's famous words are being used to "greet" visitors ("We are met"), while the epic weight of the famous speech's words give visitors a sense of the park's sacred quality as "a great battlefield." When the quotation and photograph are read together, however, they produce a decidedly different contextualization of Lincoln's words that is reminiscent of regional reconciliationist interpretations of the address. The fragment "We are met on a great battle-field" is given new meaning by its coupling with the photograph of a symbolic handshake between two aged former adversaries over the stone wall. This photograph, along with other similarly staged photographs from the battle's twenty-fifth- and fiftieth-year reunions, had become a familiar ritual of battle of Gettysburg commemoration. Photographs such as these were meant to symbolize regional reconciliation. The main photo in this collage, which also appears in another exhibit in the visitor center on the 1938 reunion, is not accompanied by any specific details about the individuals in the photo other than their identity as "Veterans at the Wall," which suggests that the veterans are symbolic "representatives" of the Union and Confederacy.

More important, the photograph helps generate the proper political and physical context for understanding Lincoln's address. The "We" that gathers "on a great battle-field" is not the original partisan Northern audience that gathered on that cold November day in 1863, nor is it the imaginary audience shared between Lincoln and park visitors that seems to be created when the quote is read in the absence of the photograph. Rather, the "We" suggests a reunited (white) nation made whole by sectional reunification. The size and prominence of the photograph suggest that neither Lincoln nor his words are the primary subjects of the collage, but instead the famous words seem to be used to add mythic weight to sectional reunion. Those not intimately familiar with Lincoln's speech can also readily interpret his utterance "We are met on a great battle-field" as a caption that records the "greeting" exchanged between the two former adversaries seventy-five years after the war. The fragment from the address, then, is used to emphasize national unity in much the same way as early twentieth-century reconciliationists pointed to the broadly ambiguous language used by Lincoln in the address as evidence that he eulogized both Union and Confederate dead.

The first collage also helps establish the appropriate physical or geographical context for understanding the address. At one level, that context seems both obvious and innocuous—since the speech was delivered in the context of the Civil War at the site of the battle of Gettysburg, then it logically follows that the line "We are met on a great battle-field" be used to create the proper geographical context for the speech. Yet the speech itself and important strands of Gettysburg Address public memory have emphasized more expansive contexts from the text other than the battle—including "the nation," "this continent," and "earth"—that promote broad reflection on various national ideals, including egalitarian American democracy and racial equality.

Rhetorical critic Edwin Black argues that the structure of the speech resembles an "hourglass" shape. The beginning and end of the speech create expansive themes, geographical references, and implied audiences, while the middle section of the address narrows considerably. The beginning of the speech is used, Black argues, to develop a "narrative of national creation" that appears to be "addressed to the ages." In these first five lines Lincoln describes the genesis of the country as "conceived in liberty, and dedicated to the proposition that all men are created equal," which are principles tested by "a great civil war." The narrative of national creation "stipulates the frame of the speech"[12] by contextualizing the Civil War within the broader history of the nation's founding principles.

The middle section narrows to the local context of the cemetery, the present moment, and the implied Gettysburg audience. This section of the address (lines 6–16, approximately), if isolated from the speech's other components, contains numerous inanimate geographical references to the "battle-field," "portion of that field," and "final resting place." Thematically, these lines consecrate the dead and inspire audiences to silently revere their sacrifices. The final lines (17–23), Black argues, are again expansive and active, as Lincoln implores the living to act as agents for future change by using the inspiration of the dead to preserve the nation and the ideals it was founded upon.

The first collage, then, brings together fragments from the middle section of the address that stress local place, time, and place with a popular photograph of reunited adversaries on the battlefield. Furthermore, because the ideology of regional reconciliation is so firmly wedded to most characterizations of Civil War battles, evocations of the battlefield context will trigger readers to recognize and create its familiar meanings of mutual valor, patriotic sacrifice, and manly courage.

Finally, the photograph takes place near the supposed "High Water Mark" of the Confederacy that was reached during the Confederates' final massive assault on the center of the Union lines at Cemetery Ridge. "Pickett's Charge," as it is commonly known, has become a national mythic tale of Southern valor in the face of insurmountable Union artillery and canister fire and, for Union supporters, the decisive turning point in the war. The Park Service considered Pickett's Charge so vital to its reconciliation message at Gettysburg that prior to opening the current visitor center in the former Gettysburg National Museum in 1989, they had located the visitor center on the battlefield overlooking Cemetery Ridge. In an ironic twist, Park Service interpretation of the assault glorified not Union victory but Southern courage. An audio station located at the Virginia Monument describes how the Confederate ranks were arranged "in perfect order, this gallant array of gallant men," as they readied for the assault. The narrator of the tape then goes on to describe the assault as a march to "eternal glory."

The Park Service's glorification of Confederate heroism was not unusual, however, and reflected Southern Lost Cause rhetoric. This rhetoric, writes Alan T. Nolan, originated in Southern rationalizations of defeat after the war, "[t]hen it spread to the North and became a national phenomenon. In the popular mind, the Lost Cause represents the national memory of the Civil War; it has been substituted for the *history* of the war."[13]

Ironically, then, the first collage appropriates Lincoln's words to comment on a symbolic act of reconciliation that took place on a part of the battlefield that has popularly commemorated Southern valor in defeat. Certain physical places, it appears, contain their own preferred commemorative meanings. In this case the "High Water Mark" functions as an anecdotal repository of Lost Cause memorializing, which helps constitute the rhetorical characteristics of regional reconciliation.

The next Park Service collage, if reading from left to right, continues to appropriate fragments from lines 6–14 of the speech: "A final resting place for those who here gave their lives that that nation might live."

The quotation used to frame this collage is obviously meant to follow the first collage, since this fragment comes from the line following the fragment used in the first collage:

6. We are met on a great battle-field of that war. We have
7. come to dedicate a portion of that field, as a final resting place
8. for those who here gave their lives that that nation might live.

With regional reconciliationist memory now intact as an interpretive frame from the first collage, visitors are invited to infer that "those who here gave their lives" are Union *and* Confederate soldiers eulogized by Lincoln. Their sacrifices, the collage suggests, were necessary to ensure "that that nation might live."

In general, the ambiguity of Lincoln's words makes it easier for various groups to appropriate their meaning. It is this middle section of the speech, however, that especially lends itself to reconciliationist interpretations of the war's causes, legacy, and deeper meanings. Garry Wills has noted that this portion of the speech resembles the section of ancient Greek funeral orations dedicated to praise for the fallen, or *epainesis*.[14] As a result, these lines stress death, sacrifice, and honorable duty, all common features of official patriotic wartime rhetoric and reconciliationist memory. In addition, this section is the most localized of the address. Its references to the battlefield and cemetery are set within a distinctive time and space, making this part more directly relevant to the Park Service's preservation of important material spaces and properties.

The distinctive rhetorical features of this section of the speech are better grasped when contrasted with the other components. Edwin Black argues, "In visual terms, the speech is like an hourglass. Temporally, it is past, present, then future. Its visceral effects are contraction, strain, and then release. Respirationally, it is an exhalation, then a pause, then an inhalation."[15] It follows, then, that the middle section of Lincoln's address represents the temporal present, a visceral "straining," and a respirational "pause." Additionally, in natal terms, the speech follows the pattern of birth, death, and rebirth, with the middle section pausing on the period of death. This section, isolated from the beginning and end, exists in a state of rhetorical inertia, a "pause" before Lincoln would exhort his audience to dedicate their futures to preserving the Union and upholding the proposition stated in the beginning that "all men are created equal."

If interpreted in conjunction with the photo of the seventy-fifth veterans' reunion, then, the recent photo of the National Cemetery in the second collage invites visitors generations removed from the war to create a memory of the Gettysburg dead as immortal and peacefully reconciled former foes instead of Union and Confederate soldiers who killed each other in battle. This clever juxtaposition insinuates not only a fraternal bond between the former adversaries but an eternal one as well.

The third and final collage continues with this address fragment: "The brave men, living and dead, who struggled here, have consecrated it, far above our poor power to add or detract." This quotation is accompanied by Matthew Brady's photograph of the wheat field where Union general John Reynolds was supposedly wounded on the first day of the battle.[16]

Brady's photograph, taken a few weeks after the battle on land that is now part of the cemetery, is a reminder that the National Cemetery is located on the battlefield. In fact, Gettysburg attorney David Wills, in consultation with then governor Andrew Curtin, selected the site because it commemorated not only sacrifice but also Union victory. Wills explained the cemetery's strategic value in a letter to Curtin: "It is the ground which formed the apex of our triangle line of battle, and the key to our line of defenses. It embraces the highest point on Cemetery Hill, and overlooks the whole battlefield. It is the spot which should be specially consecrated for this sacred purpose."[17] The collages certainly make visitors aware of the sanctification of the cemetery through martial sacrifice, but they would be hard-pressed to find information at the park about why Wills and Curtin chose to "preserve" that specific location on Cemetery Hill. Brady's wartime photograph, if placed in the first collage rather than the last, might lead visitors to more readily connect Lincoln's words to his original partisan wartime context and audience. If so, then visitors would be invited to read Lincoln's other fragments as tributes to just Union—rather than Union and Confederate—dead. Instead, the first photo helps contextualize Lincoln's address within the commemorative tradition of regional reconciliation. The second photo, a more recent color photograph of the cemetery, connects reconciliation to the present, while the final linkage between the "present" and the battlefield's "origins," represented by the third photograph, functions to preserve reconciliation as part of a fixed, "unchanging" landscape.

The entire interpretation is aided by Lincoln's words. The fragment from the final collage again stresses the battlefield as the place where soldiers sacrificed their lives for their country. The fragment "The brave men, living and dead, who struggled here, have consecrated it far above our poor power to add or detract" functions in this context to connect the origins of reconciliation to the battle of Gettysburg itself, thereby naturalizing reconciliation in the process. The coupling of the fragment with Brady's original photograph, furthermore, doubles as a subtle Park Service mission statement—the NPS respects the acts of martial sacrifice of July 1863, which have therefore consecrated the battlefield "far above *our* poor power to add or detract." Brady's photograph, juxtaposed against the second, more recent photo of the same undefiled space one hundred-plus years later, affirms the competence and credibility of the NPS as historic preservationists. So even while it utilizes one commemorative tradition to interpret Gettysburg for visitors, the Park Service asserts their neutrality and objectivity as preservationists and public historians.

The three collages are, like Lincoln's address, commemorative rather than historical. Unlike the vast majority of Park Service interpretive materials, the collages present a decontextualized and necessarily simplified rendering of Lincoln's words, delinked from their November 1863 historical context. To this commemorative and symbolic end, the collages use selected fragments from Lincoln's address in an attempt to create a timeless, inspirational message about the value of dying for one's country. Yet Lincoln also admonishes the living to continue fighting to protect the causes that the Union soldiers died for, which, as interpreted in other commemorative threads of Gettysburg Address memory, include equality and preservation of the Union and its democratic form of government. By excluding any mention of the broader causes of the war, however, the Civil War commemorative tradition of regional reconciliation necessarily creates a public memory of the Gettysburg Address as a timeless tribute to Americans who, without hesitation or the need for reflection, gave their lives for their country.

Collective Memory, Commemoration, and History

The preceding analysis of three highly visible and symbolic collages located in the main lobby of the visitor center suggests that the Park Service "preserves" the battlefield and cemetery landscape to reflect the ideals of a particular public memory of Gettysburg rather than its actual 1863 historical appearance.

Dedicated historical preservationists at the Park Service, however, would surely contend that they are not attempting to interpret the Gettysburg Address through commemoration but are simply passing along, through unbiased and accurate public history, the historical context and content of Lincoln's speech to their visitors. The Park Service's approach to public history is unquestionably fair-minded and historically accurate. In fact, their representation of the past typically follows the guidelines of history rather than commemoration, although this analysis is beginning to suggest that the Park Service, when they do rely on commemoration, can confuse it as history.

Many public memory scholars argue that history and collective memory are distinguishable. Maurice Halbwachs, for example, supports "the ultimate opposition between collective memory and history."[18] Halbwachs argues that history is something "situated external to and above groups" and remains relatively unchanged once its factual details are "fixed once and for all." History, unlike collective memory, is not affected by the social contexts of the day and utilizes evidence to achieve some degree of objectivity, while memory, according to Halbwachs, is based on how ordinary individuals conceive of the past based upon the prevailing concerns and needs of the present. Memory, furthermore, disappears when the present no longer needs to call upon the services of the past for guidance and inspiration. Conversely, history begins "when tradition ends and the social memory is fading or breaking up."[19]

Barry Schwartz argues that Halbwachs and other public memory theorists have contributed to the creation of a false dichotomy between memory and history. Pierre Nora, following Halbwachs's basic dichotomy, maintains that the contrast between history and memory is visible in the way history was used in the last third of the twentieth century to interrogate or deconstruct the past, while commemoration was used to sanctify it. According to Schwartz, Nora has helped contribute to the prevailing belief that: "History makes the past an object of analysis; commemoration makes it an object of commitment. History is a system of 'referential symbols' representing known facts about past events and their sequence; commemoration is a system of 'condensation symbols' expressing the moral sentiments these events inspire. History, like science, investigates the world by producing models of its permanence and change. Commemoration, like ideology, promotes commitment to the world by producing symbols of its values and aspirations."[20]

Schwartz argues that public memory encompasses the reciprocal relationship between history and commemoration. History, he argues, typically reflects the ideals and values that are expressed overtly in acts of commemoration; commemoration is grounded in historical fact. History, therefore, can become morally profound when it chronicles events that have deep commemorative roots, while commemoration becomes intellectually provocative when "it symbolizes values whose past existence history documents."[21]

Schwartz contends that the dichotomy created between history and memory has largely functioned to discredit memory as something "invented" or "created," with history serving a corrective role to remedy the inaccuracies and embellishments of memory. The relationship between history and memory, he argues, is reciprocal and interdependent. This relationship is evident in NPS Civil War parks in general. The NPS uses history to chronicle the factual details of the events that transpired on what is now park soil, using archaeological remains and historical records to record and "interpret" that history. Their historical accounts, however, initiated as they were during the emerging period of regional reconciliation and resurgent nationalism in the 1890s, are influenced by the prevailing commemorative values that sanctified battlefields especially as sacred shrines of national heroic sacrifice.

Upon closer inspection, each individual park can also be seen to intertwine historical and commemorative representations of the past. Yet at the level of the individual exhibit, Park Service interpretation of the past often utilizes the tools of *either* history or commemoration, although the Park Service's own commemorative voice is often masked by the overwhelming majority of exhibits devoted to historical recordings of the past. Nowhere is this clearer than in NPS Gettysburg Address interpretation. The address's historic significance is marginal in the sense that its utterance did not profoundly affect the course or outcome of the Civil War, although its commemoration has made the address a "condensation symbol" for the causes of reconciliation, progressive reform, patriotic veneration, and racial equality. The speech's symbolic value has intensified, in turn, the historiographical quest for the facts surrounding the preparation, text, and delivery of Lincoln's speech, which are painstakingly detailed throughout the park.

Unlike the commemorative collages, most of the Park Service's own interpretive materials on the Gettysburg Address are devoted to a history of the text's creation and delivery, although those factual accounts generally fit within a particular commemorative tradition. Examples of the NPS's largely historical representation of the address abound. There is a seven-paragraph description of the Gettysburg Address in the GNMP official map and guide, for example, which most visitors pick up and peruse while in the visitor center. The summary does not refer directly to any content from the speech, stating only that the address "transformed Gettysburg from a scene of carnage into a symbol, giving meaning to the sacrifice of the dead and inspiration to the living." Rather than describing what the speech meant, the brochure provides a detailed account of the events leading up to it, including two paragraphs that attempt to correct the popular "myth" that Lincoln wrote the speech on the back of an envelope during his train ride to Gettysburg: "Contrary to popular belief, Lincoln did not write the speech on the back of an envelope during the trip to Gettysburg, but took great pains in its formulation. He composed the first draft in Washington shortly before November 18 and revised it at the home of David Wills in Gettysburg sometime before the dedication. The second draft, written in ink on two pages of the same paper used for part of the first draft, reflects Lincoln's first revision of the address and, except for the words 'under God,' constitutes the text of the speech delivered at the dedication ceremony."[22] This careful reconstruction of the speech's creation is used to authenticate one version of events and discredit "popular belief." Wary of the tension between objective history and subjective belief, the Park Service does seem preoccupied with remedying false subjective accounts of the past when they fall outside their preferred commemorative framework.

The need for utilizing history to record even the most minor details surrounding the speech's creation and presentation is also magnified by the scant physical evidence of its existence, which adds to the allure and mythology of the address. The official map and guide and an interpretive marker at the site of Lincoln's speech both feature the only known photograph showing Lincoln during the dedication. Lincoln is barely recognizable in the photo, which has been altered and examined extensively to identify the historical figures, especially Lincoln, seated in the background of the photo.

The photo and accompanying wayside marker encourage visitors to connect with the past mimetically, so as to understand the precise spot where Lincoln gave his immortal speech. This marker, like much of the NPS's Gettysburg Address interpretation, uses history to describe when and where Lincoln recited his address.

Figure 1.2. Lincoln's Gettysburg Address. (Photograph courtesy of Library of Congress.)

The Gettysburg Electric Map

The Gettysburg Electric Map mixes both history and commemoration in its interpretation of the address. Many park visitors receive their most comprehensive initial orientation to GNMP from the twenty-minute Gettysburg Electric Map presentation of the battle. Taken out of service when the new visitor center opened in 2008, the map used to be the featured exhibit in the Gettysburg National Museum, owned privately by the George D. Rosensteel family until its purchase by the federal government in 1971.[23] The three-dimensional electronic map, which opened to the public in 1939, features a sound-and-light show that explains the maneuvers of each side's troops. The interpretation of the battle provided by the sound-and-light show changed little since 1939. A team of Park Service personnel reviewed the exhibit in 1979 and determined that only minor changes needed to be made. The electronic map is relevant here because it uses fragments from Lincoln's address to conclude the presentation by summarizing the historical details surrounding the dedication ceremonies of November 19 and using the address as a way to commemorate the battle.

Visitor interpretation of this conclusion, however, is influenced in large part by how the content of the presentation leading up to its ending is presented, which consists of a narrative overview of the three-day battle. The voiceover narrator uses a combination of military history and reunion sentiment to create a public memory of the battle as an important Northern victory that featured unparalleled acts of Southern bravery and heroism. Military history is used to explain the location, movements, maneuvers, and engagements between regiments, as told through the perspective of the battle's commanding generals. Reconciliationist memory, informed by Lost Cause rhetoric, is used to restore "balance" to the narrative whenever details of the battle might appear to privilege one side over the other. Descriptions of the failed Pickett's Charge, for example, are accompanied by effusive praise of Southern valor:

> The High Water Mark had been reached. Though the war would bleed on for two more years, the Confederate cause, for which her sons had fought so bravely, was doomed. The following day, July Fourth, the two armies sat, facing each other, nursing their wounds. During the evening of July 4th, in a pouring rain that must have reflected their mood, Lee, Longstreet, Ewell, Hill, Stuart—the entire Confederate army—started the withdrawal that ended the bloodiest event to ever take place on the American continent. Fifty-one thousand soldiers, Americans all, 30 percent of the armies involved, were casualties in the three days of bitter fighting. [Pause.] We direct your attention to the shape of the Union line, the famous "fishhook" formation at Gettysburg. If you keep a picture of the fishhook in your mind, you can better understand the battlefield when you make your tour.

The narrator carefully pairs comments on the Confederates' loss with praise for Southern courage. Pickett's Virginia division in particular appears to be the source of much admiration by the narrator in this exhibit and the sound-and-light show at the Cyclorama Center. Carol Reardon maintains that the heroic memory of Pickett and his men has endured largely because the Virginia press, despite their state bias, spun such convincingly detailed accounts of the battle that journalists in both the North and the South believed these accounts to be credible. Consequently, Northern readers were more likely to accept heroic characterizations of the Virginians than North Carolinians because of comparisons between the "firmness of nerve and steadiness" of Pickett's troops with the "wavering" of Pettigrew's "mostly raw" North Carolina troops by journalists such as the *Richmond Enquirer's* Jonathan Albertson.[24]

The narrator combines praise for Southern bravery with nationalistic summaries of the battle and its casualties, hinting that the two adversaries had already, by July 4 (the date mentioned twice), begun to reconcile by "facing each other" on the evening the country celebrates its national independence. The casualties, unsurprisingly, are combined from both sides to total fifty-one thousand, "all Americans," who died in the battle. The narration is also notable for its absences. Consistent with reconciliationist memory, it avoids ruminating on the larger causes, consequences, and legacies of this most decisive battle. The narrator, for example, refers only to how the Confederates fought to support their cause rather than what that cause was. The narrative then awkwardly shifts back to emphasize the centrality of the Union "fishhook" formation to help guide visitors through their battlefield tour.

After briefly summarizing the fishhook's important topography, the presentation concludes with words paraphrased from Lincoln's address: "Amid the neat rows of freshly dug graves and a few carefully chosen words of dedication, he [Lincoln] defined for all Americans the lessons of so much bloodshed. The world, he said, can never forget what they did here. It is for us to highly resolve that these dead shall not have died in vain. That this nation, under God, shall have a new birth of freedom, and that government of the people, by the people, for the people, shall not perish from the earth." Having already established the bravery and heroism of all soldiers in the battle as well as their identity as Americans, and given the narrator's assertion that Lincoln defined the lessons of the bloodshed for all Americans, the electronic map presentation invites visitors to interpret the address as a tribute to both sides of the conflict. Just as Edward Everett's fiery polemical retelling of the battle prior to Lincoln's speech was likely to alter that audience's interpretation of Lincoln's ambiguous references to "these dead" and "what they did here," so too is the map's audience likely to interpret this address fragment based on the preceding battle narrative. In this case, Lincoln's address is used to define the lessons of so much bloodshed, but those "lessons," in the context of reconciliationist memory, can be limited to battlefield behavior only since reunion sentiment sublimates consideration of either side's broader ideological motives. If, according to the Park Service's interpretation, it was how both sides fought for their cause rather than what the causes of the battle and larger war were that was important, then the only lesson that seemingly can be extracted from the address is that cause does not matter.

What matters, the presentation implies, is that all soldiers willingly and bravely sacrificed themselves for a cause that ended up saving the Union from destruction. The presentation seems to suggest that both sides fought to protect the Union, which, following the logic of the presentation, makes one wonder why a civil war was necessary in the first place. This contradiction would become blatantly obvious had the narrator directly quoted, rather than paraphrased, Lincoln's final words, especially his admonition "that from these honored dead we take increased devotion to that cause for which they gave the last full measure of devotion."

In the electronic map presentation, Lincoln's address is used to reinforce a reconciliationist public memory of the war that, without any known causes, promotes martial sacrifice and heroism for its own sake. The appropriation of the address, furthermore, is consistent with other wartime attempts to use Lincoln's final words to inspire the country to defend the nation from a foreign threat. However, when used to eulogize and honor the human sacrifices of both sides in a civil war that purportedly were necessary to preserve the life of the nation, the map ultimately reveals limits to the address's elasticity as a supportive text of reunion sentiment.

The Cyclorama and Lost Cause Memorializing

Visitors do not come into contact with NPS interpretation of the Gettysburg Address again until the sound-and-light show presented in the Cyclorama Center. This twenty-minute presentation uses Paul Philippoteaux's 360-foot painting of Pickett's Charge to tell the story of the final dramatic assault. Benjamin Dixon observes that the assault became the focal point of GNMP interpretation as early as the 1950s, which is when the NPS initiated Mission '66, a comprehensive public education program designed to extend and improve park interpretation by 1966.[25] Philippoteaux's cyclorama would be used as the centerpiece of the park's Cyclorama Visitor Center, which would be unveiled in 1962, complete with an intimate view of the High Water Mark from the center's second-floor outdoor observation deck. By 1970, Dixon writes, half of the park's recommended two-hour tour consisted of programs about the climactic Pickett's Charge, beginning with a sound-and-light tour of the cyclorama and followed by a discussion of the assault from the observation deck.

Although the Cyclorama Center is closed and no longer the centerpiece of Park Service interpretation that it once was, Philippoteaux's painting, now located in the new Museum and Visitor Center, remains a huge draw, and most visitors incorporate the sound-and-light show and the observation deck into their tour of the park.

The public memory of Pickett's Charge, as Reardon observes, has inflated its historical and military significance and overshadowed the actual events of the assault.[26] For our purposes, the memory of the assault is significant not for its inaccuracies but for the way it inculcates meanings about the war, or in this case how it functions to help visitors interpret Lincoln's speech.

Reardon argues that Pickett's Charge began its commemorative ascent in the 1890s. Representations of the assault beginning in the late nineteenth century contain, anecdotally, the themes of Southern Lost Cause memorializing, translating each retelling of Pickett's Charge into a rehearsal of the Lost Cause.

Gary W. Gallagher argues that the Lost Cause was so convincing that it "transcended region to make its way into popular American understanding."[27] Popularized nationally by films such as *Gone with the Wind* and writers like Shelby Foote, the myth, according to Alan T. Nolan, has the following "anatomy": liberty, independence, and states' rights were the causes of secession, not slavery; slaves themselves were faithful and happy; Northern abolitionists were the provocateurs; the South had not been defeated but physically overwhelmed by superior Northern resources and manpower; and the superior leadership of "saintly" generals such as Lee and Stonewall Jackson and the gallant heroics of the typical Confederate soldier compensated for the lack of resources and manpower and almost turned the war in their favor were it not for the blunders of General Longstreet at Gettysburg.[28]

Only those features of the Lost Cause myth that relate to the military history of the war make their way into NPS battlefield interpretation, however. Literary and historical representations of Pickett's Charge in the era of regional reconciliation were able to accommodate both sides honorably by telling a story of Northern victory against Southern courage and sacrifice. In the Park Service's sound-and-light program on Philippoteaux's painting of the assault, an audiotaped narrative glorifies the assault and the bravery of Lee's men. Visitors learn that fifteen thousand Confederates on a mile-long front marched across the fields under heavy artillery fire and then, as the Rebels approached the Angle, endured canister fire that created a "hail of death." Despite the unrelenting bombardment, the Confederates kept coming; Confederate general Lewis Armistead was fatally wounded at the Angle as he led a final desperate surge over the stone wall. "Pickett's Charge," the narrator concludes, "one of the most courageous attacks in military history, has run its course to a high-water mark of valor and devotion, and of those who came across that field, two out of three will not return." As if to lend the point some historical credibility, the tape concludes by suggesting that Lincoln's Gettysburg Address reinforced the notion that "ALL who fought here, North AND South, gained imperishable glory."

Representations of Pickett's Charge such as this were invaluable to reconciliationist memory because they provided an interpretive space for both white Northerners and Southerners to recognize their own "imperishable glory" while casting the other in respectable and admired tones. Northerners, for example, can savor the fruits of a decisive victory while simultaneously creating a memory of Rebels as soldiers who passively and sacrificially walked across the open fields under heavy fire to endure a brave and gallant death, as opposed to men who actively sought to "kill" Union troops and destroy the Union. Southerners, meanwhile, can take some measure of comfort in retellings of this defeat by creating Lost Cause memories of losing to overpowering Northern technology (stories of the assault like the Park Service's typically represent the Union through its weapons as agents, rather than specific troops) instead of superior courage or strategic acumen.

Figure 1.3. General John F. Reynolds Memorial. (Photograph by Don Wiles, donated to public domain.)

The Gettysburg National Cemetery

The Park Service does influence interpretation of the Gettysburg Address in the Soldiers' National Cemetery, but veterans' groups and sculptors who funded and designed the cemetery's various memorials also share that task. Today's visitors are encouraged to make their final stop of the recommended tour at the cemetery, which until the 1960s was the most popular stop for American visitors and remains so today for foreign tourists.[29] The cemetery includes the graves of over six thousand soldiers, including almost four thousand Union bodies reburied between October 1863 and March 1864; the Soldiers' National Monument, dedicated in 1869; the monument to Major General John F. Reynolds, the highest-ranking Union officer killed at Gettysburg; and the Gettysburg Address Memorial, dedicated in 1912 (see figure 1.3).

The Soldiers' National Cemetery began initially as a regional project coordinated by the state of Pennsylvania. Intended to honor the heroism of Union soldiers, the cemetery did not include the bodies of Confederate soldiers killed at Gettysburg until the early twentieth century. The cemetery contains a more circular design compared to the linear structure of the battlefield tour, which gives visitors more control over interpreting the cemetery grounds. NPS interpretation within the cemetery is limited to a few directional signs and field markers, which cumulatively function to historicize the cemetery. The overwhelming feeling of the cemetery is commemorative, however, which ultimately provides visitors with the opportunity to create much broader symbolic connections between the past and present.

Abraham Lincoln is a central commemorative subject in the cemetery today. The Lincoln Address Memorial, unveiled in 1912 in time for the 50th Anniversary Reunion of the Blue and Gray, is a popular first stop for visitors once on cemetery grounds. The context surrounding the memorial invites visitors to draw upon two conflicting funereal traditions to help interpret the address. The eminent horticulturist William Saunders designed the cemetery in the nineteenth-century tradition of the pastoral and "romantic" rural cemetery. Popularized first by the Mount Auburn Cemetery dedicated in Cambridge in 1831, the rural cemetery was rapidly duplicated in cities like Pittsburgh, Philadelphia, and New York. Inspired by people such as Henry David Thoreau, "Romanticists," according to Richard Morris, rejected the gloomy, foreboding religious urban cemeteries that made death seem fearful and unnatural. In their place Romanticists created green pastoral cemeteries with exotic shrubs, trees, flowers, and bushes that stressed the interrelationship between death and nature.[30] According to Blanche LindenWard, places like Mount Auburn "presented visitors with a programmed sequence of sensory experiences, primarily visual, intended to elicit specific emotions, especially the so-called pleasures of melancholy that particularly appealed to contemporary romantic sensibilities."[31]

The Soldiers' National Cemetery today still resembles the rural cemetery of the Romanticists in its basic landscape design. The Park Service has marked, for example, the various Norway maple trees, evergreens, and arborvitae that were part of Saunders's original plan. Benches still encircle the cemetery, enabling visitors to stop and reflect. Large pines still isolate the grounds of the cemetery from the rest of the battlefield, enhancing its rural isolation.

Morris argues that by the end of the nineteenth century "Heroists" had successfully altered the intention and design of the rural cemetery to reflect the ideology of their followers. Heroists eschewed the easy sentimentalism of the Romanticists and their improper displays of public affection. The rural cemeteries, they believed, were overly adorned, pastoral, and individualistic. Heroists believed that the Romanticists used language too freely to express their emotions. Language is the servant of the emotions and impedes action and accomplishment, two cherished ideals of the Heroic tradition. Heroists believed that accomplishments were measured by acts of stoic determination and courage, and what needed to be memorialized in stone were not the words or sentiments of death but reminders of heroic actions.[32]

Heroists tended to equate a memorial's size with the accomplishments of the individual; therefore, high-ranking leaders were often memorialized by large, unadorned granite obelisks that completely rejected the artistic and sentimental Romanticist memorial style. The prototype obelisk is the Washington Monument. Morris writes that:

> Measuring more than 555 feet from the ground to its crown, this white marble shaft, which was begun in 1848, does not invite viewers to contemplate nature or art or one's "finer sentiments." One need not indulge in fanciful psychologizing about its phallic appearance to recognize that this memorial is an accomplishment of labor rather than of artistic skill, that it equates size with significance, that it asserts its dominance over the environment, over nature— that it speaks of *power over,* of control. Rather than being an expression of a need to live in harmony with that against which all things are measured from the Romanticist perspective, a structure of such monumental proportions announces both the dominance of the species over nature and the consequences of Heroist immortality.[33]

The Soldiers' National Cemetery does not contain obelisks the size of the Washington Monument, of course, but its grounds contain numerous examples of heroic memorials (the battlefield itself contains hundreds) that generate cumulative messages about the desirability of power, action, and self-control. The memorial to Union general John Reynolds is one clear example. A life-sized statue of Reynolds, funded by members of Reynolds's staff and dedicated in 1872, is the first bronze statue of an individual at Gettysburg and sits atop a column measuring fifteen feet tall. Reynolds, who was killed at Gettysburg, appears steady and determined. His position of power and control is communicated by the size and height of his statue as well as his fixed gaze. Reynolds, with field glasses in hand, exudes power that is most closely associated with his omniscient stare over the battlefield (and visitors' heads), granting him command over the battlefield terrain and his men.

Romanticist and Heroic memorial traditions would appear to invite visitors to create different interpretations of Lincoln's Gettysburg Address. The Heroic memorials, however, might carry greater rhetorical sway in the cemetery because their meanings closely parallel the Park Service's own interpretation of the battle and address.

The historical form of Park Service interpretive markers at the cemetery is different than the Heroist memorials, although their meanings are strikingly similar. An interpretive marker located at the base of the Gettysburg Address Memorial provides a narrative summary of the consecration of the cemetery that contains the same Heroist skepticism of the connection between language and emotional reflection about death:

We are met on a great battle-field of that war. We are met to dedicate a portion of it as the final resting-place of those who have given their lives that that nation might live.

President Abraham Lincoln
Gettysburg Address

On the morning of November 19, 1863, nearly 20,000 statesmen, soldiers, and citizens converged on this hill to consecrate the new Soldiers' National Cemetery. The speakers' platform was located in Evergreen Cemetery to your left.

The Hon. Edward Everett, principal speaker and former Governor of Massachusetts, took the platform at noon. His eloquent, but exhausting, speech lasted two hours.

Following a hymn, President Abraham Lincoln rose to deliver "dedicatory remarks." As the crowd strained to see and hear, Lincoln spoke deliberately and without gestures. According to some observers, the people received his prayer-like words in stunned silence. The "Gettysburg Address" lasted two minutes.

Lincoln left the platform believing his remarks had disappointed the people. As time passed, however, it became clear that his simple utterances had found a place in many American hearts— and would for generations to come.

This straightforward chronicle of the day's dedication ceremonies indicates that Lincoln's address was profoundly moving. The selection of quotations and facts gives the impression of being informative, but the marker actually says little about what Lincoln spoke about or why people found the speech so moving compared to Everett's address. The narrative, oddly, seems remarkably evasive about the content of this legendary speech, preferring instead to stress Lincoln's style and delivery.

At the same time, however, the marker's simple prose and hourly chronicle of the day's events does appear to create an objective point of view. As Peter Novick argues, even history that seems "objective" by the standards of most professional historians at the time can prove, upon later reflection, to have been driven by the subtle interpretation of historical facts. The writing of Civil War history beginning in the 1880s and 1890s, he asserts, contributed and conformed to the growing demands for white sectional reconciliation through "balanced" histories of the war that carefully avoided placing undue praise or criticism on either side.[34]

This marker appears to have been written with the same precision and restraint so as to avoid communicating anything about the partisan sentiments that certainly impassioned the thousands of Union supporters that November day or the tremendous grief that accompanied the occasion and the war itself. This marker creates the deceptive impression that the key events of the consecration are being "interpreted" for public consumption, while what is really being shared are inconsequential facts that reveal little about the speech and why it has had such a profound effect on audiences in America and abroad.

The Heroist memorial tradition, then, coheres with a reconciliationist public memory of the war. Reconciliationist memory creates a context for describing the heroic and valorous deeds of common soldiers from both the Union and Confederate ranks during the course of battle, while heroic memorials, through their funereal tributes to the dead, preserve reconciliationist memory's need to repress discourse about the causes of war or the sorrowful meanings of death.

The New Museum and Visitor Center

The National Park Service unveiled its new $103 million Gettysburg Museum and Visitor Center in April 2008. The 139,000-square-foot complex, which resembles a renovated Pennsylvania farmstead featuring recycled barn timbers and a granite exterior, is part of a $125 million campaign designed to restore key portions of the battlefield to their original 1863 appearance while situating the three-day battle within a broader historical context that includes slavery as its primary cause and racial equality as its principal legacy.[35]

The old visitor center was constructed on a portion of the Army of the Potomac's defensive lines on Cemetery Ridge, which "was right in the middle of what we were trying to preserve and protect," according to supervisory historian Scott Hartwig.[36] The new complex, located away from the battle lines in a hollow about two-thirds of a mile from the original center, includes 24,000 feet of new exhibit space; two 187-seat, three-screen theaters; and a gallery designed as a round barn that houses artist Paul Philippoteaux's renovated 377-foot-long mural completed in 1884.[37]

Developed in partnership with the nonprofit Gettysburg Foundation, Gettysburg's massive overhaul is driven by a mix of traditional battlefield preservation and new interpretive imperatives largely unburdened from the strictures of interpreting only preserved landscapes.[38] The NPS began its most recent refurbishment of the battlefield by burying electrical lines along Emmitsburg Road in the early 1990s, then demolishing the massive observation tower in 2000 that both rested upon and surveyed the battlefield. More recently, the Park Service has removed trees and installed fences in order to restore the battle's original sightlines and intends to tear down the original visitor center and the Cyclorama Center, both of which are situated on the original battlefield.

While it looks backward to preserve the Pennsylvania farmland to its wartime appearance, the new visitor center attempts to be forward thinking in its interpretation of Gettysburg's role in American history. For example, almost two-thirds of the new 24,000-square-foot exhibit space is devoted to themes other than the three-day battle, including broader ruminations on slavery, westward expansion, the contested 1860 presidential election, and the postwar struggle for racial equality. "For a lot of our visitors," explained the Park Service's Katie Lawhon, "this is their Civil War experience. It's our one and only chance to tell the story right. We don't want people thinking the war was one three-day battle."[39]

The visitor center's dozen new exhibits and twenty-two-minute orientation film *A New Birth of Freedom* reflect the agency's commitment to including African Americans as part of the war's broader story and legacy. The widespread diffusion of emancipationist memory at Gettysburg Museum and Visitor Center raises compelling questions about its coexistence with reconciliationist memories embedded within battlefield interpretation: Does the coexistence of emancipationist and reconciliationist commemorative traditions make Gettysburg National Military Park a contested site of public memory? Does a powerful new emancipationist framing of the war at the Museum and Visitor Center provide visitors with the knowledge required to make visible remnants of reconciliationist memory at GNMP that helped sublimate racial equality as one of the war's unfinished legacies for so many years? Or, conversely, are African Americans' wartime sacrifices folded into a more inclusive and harmonious version of interracial reconciliationist memory that praises the valor of all men who gave their lives in the service of their respective causes? If so, will an ideology of (interracial) heroic masculinity continue to invite visitors to identify with the war's romantic pathos rather than question the centrality of its savage violence? *A New Birth of Freedom,* narrated by Morgan Freeman, offers a condensed glimpse into the Park Service's revised framing of Gettysburg and Civil War memory that reverberates throughout the $103 million complex and provides some tentative answers to the questions that will continue to shape Civil War battlefield preservation and interpretation for years to come.

The film is divided into seven parts. The first two examine slavery's role in leading to war; the three middle sections summarize the three days of battle at Gettysburg; and the final two parts explore Lincoln's Gettysburg Address, appropriating its concluding passages to commemorate the sacrifices at Gettysburg that inspired "a new birth of freedom" for formerly enslaved African Americans and "ever broadening groups of citizens."

A New Birth of Freedom resolves a dramatic tension between slavery and freedom through Gettysburg's symbolization of a transformative war that engendered a slow but inexorable commitment to freedom, which the film defines as the extension of full citizenship to all Americans. The film's initial framing of freedom as the antithesis of chattel slavery ("In the balance hangs the future of slavery in this country, and the future of freedom") helps viewers interpret the film's use of concluding passages from Lincoln's address ("We here highly resolve that these dead shall not have died in vain—that this nation, under God, shall have a new birth of freedom—and that government of the people, by the people, for the people, shall not perish from the earth") as calling for a renewed commitment to racial equality.

Reflecting the status quo for generations of post–Civil War Americans, the Park Service used Lincoln's address in its previous visitor center and in other park exhibits as an eloquent expression of white regional reconciliation. Dedicated primarily to interpreting the battle of Gettysburg, the lines (6–15) from Lincoln's address that refer to the temporal present and the spatial context of the cemetery were used in Park Service exhibits to express reunionist sentiments about the manly courage and sacrifice of white Northern and Southern common soldiers alike.

These older exhibits lead one to conclude that the Park Service is constrained against appropriating an emancipationist interpretation of the address because it would disrupt a dominant public memory of the war as a depoliticized conflict between white "brothers" of the North and South who fought with equal valor for their unnamed cause. The new film and exhibits, however, deftly sidestep this dilemma by again linking the South and North together, this time through criticism of their widespread racism and complicity in benefiting economically from slavery. The iconic Lincoln, meanwhile, seems to be the one unifying figure throughout the film's chronology that viewers can trust, and even though it identifies emancipation as a politically expedient act, *A New Birth* nevertheless grants Lincoln the space to define Gettysburg as the event that would threaten, and then affirm, the nation's dedication to freedom.

While these interpretations are new at Gettysburg National Military

Park, white and black leaders had been using the Gettysburg Address to produce readings of Lincoln as a prophet of racial integration and equality since the 1960s.[40] In his Civil War Centennial Address, for example, Pennsylvania governor William Scranton exclaimed: "Today, our nation is still engaged in a test to determine if the United States, conceived in liberty and dedicated to the proposition that all men are created equal, can long endure. Blood has been shed in the dispute over the equality of men even in 1963."[41] Scranton and many others made it appear as if Lincoln argued in his speech that the fate of the country would depend on its ability to forge a lasting racial equality.

Despite the growing popularity of a public memory of the address as a manifesto of racial equality, this interpretation was far from universal in the 1960s. While some saw the speech as a rationale for individual rights, others continued to insist that the address function as an inspiration for patriotic veneration, national sacrifice, and (white) reconciliation. The theme of regional reconciliation was still predominant, for example, in the U.S. government's centennial commemoration of the Civil War in the early 1960s.[42] White regional reconciliation was rarely made explicit in official commemorations of the war but becomes discernible through the absence of black voices and perspectives.

Healing and unification are clearly the most dominant meanings that arose from interpretations of the Gettysburg Address during the 1960s, although groups placed different regional and racial boundaries around that inclusiveness. By the 1990s it was becoming more common to interpret the speech as utterly transcendent, with many seeing as its purpose the healing of both racial and regional discord, although this helped mask the contradictory relationship between regional and racial reconciliation. Barry Schwartz argues that Garry Wills's 1992 Pulitzer Prize–winning *Lincoln at Gettysburg* is so broadly appealing because it affirms the egalitarian mood of late twentieth-century America. Schwartz states that Wills's interpretation of a "touching speech that pays tribute to both combatants, North and South, as it affirms the equality of all men, black and white, makes sense in a postmodernizing society in which boundarylessness is idealized. Convincing so many that Lincoln made such a speech, Garry Wills has produced a symbol for his generation."[43]

An interpretation of Gettysburg as a climactic challenge to the nation's commitment to freedom, now safely enmeshed as part of the status quo, can assume the status of a naturalized rendering of events at Gettysburg's new Museum and Visitor Center. At one level, it would be easy to criticize the Park Service for its belated revisionism, although the agency acknowledges it is reactive to changes in historical scholarship initiated by academics with more financial support and training.[44] To their credit, however, many personnel have lobbied for years to make its exhibits more inclusive, although budget restrictions have made such changes prohibitive. Perhaps it is fair to say that the agency could have been (and still could be) more reflexive about its own role in perpetuating a racially exclusive memory of the war that it now deems antiquated. While it might be unrealistic to expect the agency to reference its own duplicity in sublimating racial equality as one of the war's unfinished legacies, such contradictions are now visible at Gettysburg, a site of essentially contested memory where visitors can see field markers, monuments, and waysides that venerate the men whose racism is now the subject of criticism at the Visitor and Museum Center. That discontinuity should generate lively debate at Gettysburg in the years ahead, opening the site to healthy "interpretation debates" that could accelerate new ways of envisaging the instructiveness of public memory.

2

Reviving Emancipationist Memory at Harpers Ferry National Historical Park

The rhetorical dimensions of Civil War memory are most salient in struggles to assess the nature and extent of racial inclusion and equality in America.[1] The popular "reconciliationist" memory became so dominant by century's end that it seemed transcendent, creating feelings of national unity despite its exclusion of other war memories.

Largely eliminated from historical consciousness was an "emancipationist" memory of the war. This emancipationist memory was commonly voiced by African Americans in the late nineteenth and early twentieth centuries to reinforce a memory of the war as a Union victory whose spoils included the liberation of black Americans. Yet by the time of the Spanish-American War the country was so awash with what Nina Silber calls the "romance of reunion" that the concern for black equality became known as the failed radical experiment of Reconstruction.[2]

Harpers Ferry, the site of John Brown's attempted slave rebellion in 1859 that helped stir up sectional hostilities to a boiling point, stands at the center of memories about the war's causes and legacy. Visitors at Harpers Ferry National Historical Park (HFNHP) only have to cross the street from the site of Brown's raid on the Federal Arsenal to observe an example of the active struggle over Brown's memory. A monument funded in 1905 by the United Daughters of the Confederacy (UDC) dedicated to Heyward Shepherd, the first person killed in Brown's raid, utilizes a Southern Lost Cause perspective to interpret the raid, while an interpretive marker created by the Park Service in the mid-1990s located next to the monument is a rejoinder to the monument from the perspective of emancipationist memory.

Shepherd, a black freeman employed by the Baltimore and Ohio Railroad Company at the time of the insurrection, was caught in the crossfire between Brown's raiders and local townspeople and militia after stepping off his railway car late in the evening of October 16, 1859.[3] The UDC's monument to Shepherd resembles, at first glance, countless tributes to those who sacrificed their lives in acts of selfless duty to defend honorable causes. Identifying Shepherd as an "industrious and respected colored freeman," the monument praises Shepherd's selfless actions on that fateful evening "in pursuance of his duties as an employee of the Baltimore and Ohio Railroad Company." Upon closer inspection, the monument resembles a typical Southern Lost Cause interpretation of blacks as inferior but subservient people complacent with the slave system.[4] The monument, one of only a few artifacts in the town not created by the NPS, continues by praising the "character and faithfulness" of Shepherd and "thousands of Negroes who, under many temptations throughout subsequent years of war, so conducted themselves that no stain was left upon a record which is the peculiar heritage of the American people."[5]

At the base of the monument is an interpretive marker, written by the Park Service in 1996, that includes this commentary on the Heyward Shepherd monument:

HARPERS FERRY HISTORY
Another Perspective:

In 1932, W. E. B. DuBois, founder of the Niagara Movement, and a founder of the National Association for the Advancement of Colored People (NAACP), responded to the Shepherd monument by penning these words:

Here
John Brown
Aimed at Human Slavery
A Blow
That woke a guilty nation
With him fought
Seven slaves and sons of slaves
Over his crucified corpse
Marched 200,000 black soldiers
And 4,000,000 freedmen
Singing

"John Brown's body lies a mouldering in the grave
But his soul goes marching on!"

———————————

Located just a few yards from the Federal Arsenal, the Shepherd monument attempts to forget slavery by ignoring Brown and his raid altogether, while the Park Service's interpretive marker uses Brown's raid to remember slavery as an important cause of the Civil War. The Shepherd monument and accompanying NPS "Harpers Ferry History" interpretive marker demonstrate that conflicts over Civil War memory are active at HFNHP, and the Park Service, by owning the space where Brown's raid took place, plays an important role in shaping its meaning.[6]

In this chapter I explore further the changing dynamics of race, memory, and identity as they are created through HFNHP interpretive exhibits devoted to John Brown's attempted slave insurrection and its legacy. Like the Shepherd monument and adjoining NPS exhibit, these dynamics are best observed through the interplay between older and recent interpretation, dominant and marginal Civil War memories, mimetic and symbolic styles of interpretation, and history and myth as genres of memory used to lend credibility and coherence to interpretation.[7]

Incorporated into the National Park system in 1944, HFNHP creates two broadly different interpretations of the town's meaning and legacy. Exhibits created in two different time periods, the late 1960s and the mid-1990s, help account for these divergent interpretations. Exhibits created in the 1960s are typically devoted to chronicling the history of preserved material structures dating back to the town's Civil War era, a periodization justified by Brown's 1859 raid and the town's strategic importance during the Civil War. The goals and values of preservation overwhelm and dominate interpretation in these earlier exhibits. Thus the "lived" history of important physical structures is featured prominently in older exhibits, thereby "dehumanizing" the town's memory and implicitly placing the Park Service in the role of heroic preservationist.

If earlier interpretive exhibits were shaped by the goals and standards of historic preservation, more recent exhibits interpret Harpers Ferry's history as symbolically constitutive of emerging black equality in America. Recent exhibits, influenced by the at one time radical "emancipationist" memory[8] of the Civil War expressed by black leaders such as Frederick

Douglass and W.E.B. DuBois, are so pervasive and widespread across the park that their sheer volume threatens to subsume other interpretations of Harpers Ferry created through older exhibits.[9] The emancipationist memory, furthermore, is used to reinforce a national mythic narrative of inexorable progress and inserts Brown, Douglass, and DuBois in particular into the hero roles of that narrative. Interpretation itself is wrested loose from preservation in these exhibits, allowing a more active space for visitors to observe the vibrancy of the past and its influence in the present, especially compared to older exhibits that elevate the Park Service to the role of expert preservationists.[10]

The vast majority of park interpretation is concentrated in Lower Town Harpers Ferry, which consists of a cluster of outdoor exhibits and indoor museums located near the Federal Arsenal's site at the time of Brown's raid. The town's heaviest pedestrian traffic is centered in this part of town, reflecting Lower Town's density of park interpretation, retail shops, and restaurants. I concentrate my analysis on Park Service interpretation found in Lower Town, including outdoor interpretive markers written in the late 1960s located along the Shenandoah River and near the arsenal and indoor exhibits from the John Brown Museum completed in the mid-1990s.

Park Exhibits at Virginius Island

The story of John Brown's attempted slave rebellion anchors HFNHP's overall narrative. The action of the Harpers Ferry story, with Brown at its center, took place at the Federal Armory and Arsenal, located at the confluence of the Potomac and Shenandoah rivers in Lower Town adjacent to a stretch of land along the Shenandoah known as Virginius Island.

The town of Harpers Ferry experienced rapid economic growth in the decades leading up to Brown's attempted insurrection due largely to the rapid production of weapons. Concerned about potential threats from its southern, western, and northern borders, the U.S. Congress passed legislation to establish armories for the manufacture and storage of arms in 1794. At the time, George Washington was determined to build an armory at Harpers Ferry based on its proximity to Washington and its powerful water current as a source of energy for weapon production. The pace of weapon manufacturing skyrocketed in the early 1900s after John Hall came to Harpers Ferry from Maine and standardized the production of weapons with interchangeable parts. By 1861 the armory had produced over six hundred thousand muskets, rifles, and pistols, and employed over four hundred workers, or nearly one-third of the town's population, leading many to refer to Harpers Ferry simply as an armory town.[11]

Seven interpretive markers describe the armory's history, each located about one hundred feet apart on a narrow stretch of land separating Shenandoah Street and the Shenandoah River. These markers, written in the late 1960s, reflect a tone of detachment and concern for historical accuracy, a common feature of interpretive efforts during this period. Although the NPS has always associated preservation with interpretation, earlier efforts confined interpretation to brief, literal descriptions of the material history of a preserved structure. By imagining what a given building, fort, or battlefield looked like years earlier, visitors are therefore invited to construct shared memories mimetically as opposed to the more abstract symbolic memorializing typical of recently completed exhibits. The following interpretive marker is representative of this preservationist perspective:

ARSENAL BUILDINGS

Two brick arsenal buildings, which once housed about 100,000 weapons produced at the Harpers Ferry Armory, occupied these grounds.

Capture of the firearms was the objective of John Brown's 1859 raid.

Eighteen months after Brown's attack, the Civil War erupted. When Virginia militia advanced on the town on April 18, 1861, an outnumbered Federal garrison burned the arsenal and evacuated the town. The buildings and nearly 15,000 guns were destroyed.

The arsenal buildings begin and end as the subject of this marker, thus inviting visitors to retrace the buildings' structural changes in that physical space. Interpretation would appear somewhat limited at this site, as the marker brackets the buildings' origin and eventual destruction and shuts off any larger meanings the site might have to offer, especially with regard to the arsenal's impact on people. Hardly a conscious effort by the Park Service to limit visitor interpretations of the arsenal buildings, the marker is more revealing as evidence of how thoroughly Park Service preservation goals had enveloped and defined interpretation by this time period. The result is a mimetic form whose rhetorical structure helps facilitate and satiate a concern for accurate and literal representations of the material past.

The 1960s: "Dehumanizing" the Memory of John Brown's Raid

Pre-1960s: Competing Memories of Brown's Raid

Outdoor interpretive markers pertaining to Brown's raid from the 1960s tend to "dehumanize" the past by interpreting the history of the arsenal building's preservation rather than the legacy of Brown himself. The potential of Brown's raid for sparking intense and conflicting symbolic memories is evidenced by public discourse in the weeks between Brown's capture and execution. Bertram Wyatt-Brown writes that newspapers across the divided nation constructed various images of Brown, "whether as saint, as Whig patriot upholding the true meaning of the American Revolution, as an avenging instrument of an Old Testament God, or as a terrorist leader of black insurgency."[12]

Broad consensus over the meaning of Brown's raid and the nature of his personality was rare, even among Brown's fellow abolitionists, especially in the six weeks between the raid and Brown's hanging. Abolitionists who supported the practice of moral suasion, such as William Lloyd Garrison, decried the violent aspirations of Brown and his followers while simultaneously likening the raiders' objectives to the 1776 revolutionaries' struggle for freedom. Other pacifist abolitionists such as Wendell Phillips initially distanced themselves from Brown, only to later praise him as a brave martyr for the antislavery cause. Brown won their support after it became clear through the widely published letters and statements that accompanied his trial that he was proving to be an eloquent advocate of the antislavery cause.[13]

Many black abolitionists, meanwhile, as well as blacks in general, praised Brown's actions, although they were more likely than white abolitionists to observe the strategic failure of Brown's raid. David Littlefield argues that African Americans, as a result of their direct experiences with slavery, favored a more pragmatic approach to eliminating the institution, preferring swift and decisive action over abstract, moral denouncements of slavery. White abolitionists, Littlefield argues, relied on their idealism to criticize slavery, denouncing the institution on moral grounds and using moral suasion to alter public attitudes and legislation about slavery rather than supporting more aggressive forms of resistance.[14] And so while most African Americans honored Brown's sacrifice, they also expressed frustration with his planning and execution of the raid, including his reluctance to share orders with his fellow raiders and his alleged indecisiveness inside the arsenal, which created delays that had fatal consequences for several of Brown's men.

White abolitionists, then, were more apt and willing to spread a symbolic memory of Brown as Christlike martyr whose sacrifice would aid the moral cause of abolition. Many blacks, meanwhile, while appreciative of Brown's sacrifice, were more likely to regard other more practical and strategically successful forms of resistance, such as Nat Turner's slave rebellion, as a more effective critique of slavery.

Southern fire-eaters labeled Brown a madman, assassin, and "misled fanatic," while more moderate Southern unionists decried the raid but minimized its importance by mocking the ineptitude of Brown and his raiders as military strategists and pointing out the overall failure of Brown's mission to inspire a slave rebellion.[15] Northern and Southern moderates also tried to minimize the raid's effects on growing sectional hostilities by downplaying its symbolism. Northern and Southern politicians, according to Marouf Hasian Jr., accomplished this by evaluating Brown's assault within the context of existing state and federal "public" laws rather than giving credence to Brown's claims that he was acting to free the slaves as an agent of God's "natural" laws.[16] Of course, moderate Northern and Southern politicians evaluated the legality of Brown's raid differently. Southerners were quick to see Brown as guilty of murder, treason, and insurrection, while moderate Northern politicians, including President James Buchanan, often deferred to Virginia state law and the civility and reasonableness of legal due process in general. From this "sentimental" moderate perspective, writes Hasian, "Brown's radicalism and extremism could not be aesthetically appealing until it had been sanitized, cleansed of its anarchism before it could be considered to be a legitimate part of any reforms."[17]

Brown himself was unequivocal about the righteousness of his raid as the enactment of a sacred "natural" law, endowed by God, that gave all people the right to live a life free from bondage. Brown's perspective became quite clear in the weeks following his raid, largely because Virginia governor Henry A. Wise provided a platform for Brown's martyrdom by granting reporters open access to Brown while also allowing him to correspond freely with family, friends, and political supporters. Brown biographer Stephen B. Oates writes of this exchange between Brown and several reporters and bystanders, Governor Wise, and other officers and politicians:

> A bystander interrupted. "Do you consider this a religious movement?"
>
> "It is, in my opinion, the greatest service man can render to God."
>
> "Do you consider yourself an instrument in the hands of Providence?"
>
> "I do."
>
> "Upon what principle do you justify your acts?"
>
> "Upon the Golden Rule. I pity the poor in bondage that have none to help them: that is why I am here; not to gratify any personal animosity, revenge, or vindictive spirit. It is my sympathy with the oppressed and the wronged, that are as good as you and as precious in the sight of God."[18]

For Brown, a strict Calvinist, the laws he obliged were natural ones, and they transcended the rights and freedoms expressed in the public laws of the day. As Hasian observes, one reporter at Brown's trial exclaimed, "he recklessly transgresses all positive law and only recognizes as binding what he considers to be God's command."[19] For Brown, the time between his capture and execution was an opportunity to outline and cement an interpretation of his raid as a prophetic symbol of widespread bloodshed designed to liberate slaves.

Interpretations of Brown's raid as symbolically significant also hinged on defining Brown as sane at the time of the attack. Those who defined

Brown as insane tended to be friends, family, and lawyers who wanted to save him from execution, Northern abolitionists tied to Brown who were fearful of Virginia prosecution, and Northern and Southern moderates concerned that the attempted insurrection would lead to disunion. Although keeping Brown alive, avoiding prosecution, and quelling sectional hostilities were some of the more immediate pragmatic justifications for arguing Brown's insanity, the long-term consequences of an insanity interpretation on the public memory of Brown's raid were also profound. Specifically, it would mean understanding Brown's raid as an isolated act of violence from a madman whose actions bore no connection to any broader social and political contexts and institutions of that era.[20]

Brown himself, of course, rejected the insanity defense proffered by his lawyers and in its place offered an eloquent, if often contradictory, biblical defense of his actions, knowing full well that his martyrdom depended, in addition to his execution, on Northern interpretations of his raid as heroic and, above all, rational. Virginia's Governor Wise, who needed good publicity from the trial to generate support for a fledgling Democratic presidential nomination bid, appeased many angry Southerners by rejecting the insanity defense and thereby hastening Brown's execution but in the process praised aspects of Brown's "rational" persona and contributed to his martyrdom. "They are themselves mistaken who take [Brown] to be a madman," exclaimed Wise, in a comment that was widely published during the trial. "He is a bundle of the best nerves I ever saw cut and thrust and bleeding and in bonds. He is cool, collected, and indomitable."[21]

Brown and Wise, writes Robert E. Mcglone, while trial adversaries, shared equally in their dramatization of the raid and exaggeration of its far-reaching impact on slave insurrection, each using the event to fan the flames of sectional hostility in support of their own political and moral aspirations. Both men, while interpreting the raid differently, contributed to its dramatic symbolism, thereby helping to ensure that its legacy would transcend Harpers Ferry and make its way into Civil War and American history generally.

Insane terrorist. Old Testament prophet. Martyr of black emancipation. Whig patriot. These labels, among others, helped structure different groups' interpretations of Brown's raid in its aftermath, and while brandishing such labels might appear to serve more overt rhetorical purposes in the Civil War era, its influence might seem less relevant today. The politics of Brown's legacy, however, are still important, especially as they relate to issues of racial diversity, the struggle for equality, and the use of violence as a vehicle for social change. These politics are implicitly reflected in the legacy accorded to Brown by different historians. Some historians of the "needless (civil) war" school such as Allan Nevins, for example, said of the raid: "Nothing in the logic of forces or events required so crazy an act."[22] Although Nevins questions Brown's sanity and that of a public that accepts Brown's act as a necessary and inevitable precursor to a "just" Civil War, other historians argue that history can only hold a place for Brown if his raid is connected to other social and political currents of his, and our, time.[23]

The broad range of available interpretations of Brown and his raid on Harpers Ferry's arsenal would seem to make it difficult for the Park Service to "preserve" a single interpretation of Brown's legacy. Moreover, some interpretive choices would appear to be more controversial than others. The raid, for example, could be interpreted as a form of resistance used to inspire the movement toward black emancipation and, eventually, black equality. This interpretation, however, while adhering to the familiar Park Service theme of progressive history, would likely implicitly endorse domestic terror as a means of resistance. Casting Brown as a martyr would also seem to encourage park visitors to connect Brown's religious theology with federal laws of racial equality, placing church and state in a more symbiotic relationship than is customary. The NPS could also attempt to avoid more obvious controversy by downplaying the radicalism and extremism of Brown and his raid—much as pro-union moderates did during Brown's trial—which would encourage a more "sentimental" representation of Brown's anarchy.

The 1960s: "John Brown's Fort" Interpretive Markers

The Park Service certainly cannot be accused of avoiding Brown, as he is the main thematic focus of the exhibits at HFNHP. Two museums are devoted to Brown and his legacy, while several others use his raid as a point of departure to describe other developments in American society. There are also several outdoor interpretive markers located just northeast of Virginius Island and near the arsenal's original location at the time of Brown's raid. These exhibits, such as the text from one of these reproduced below from John Brown's Fort, describe Brown and his raid:

JOHN BROWN FORT

Here is a building with a curious past. Since its construction in 1848, it has been vandalized, dismantled, and moved four times—all because of its fame as John Brown's stronghold.

The Fort's "Movements"

1848	Built as fire engine house for U. S. Armory.
1859	Serves a stronghold for John Brown and his raiders.
1861–1865	Escapes destruction during Civil War (only armory building to do so), but is vandalized by souvenir-hunting Union and Confederate soldiers and later travelers.
1891	Dismantled and transported to Chicago Exposition.
1895	Rescued from conversion to stable and brought back to Harpers Ferry area to be exhibited on a farm.
1909	Purchased by Storer College and moved on campus.
1968	Moved by National Park Service to within 150 feet of its original location.

This exhibit, written during the same time period as the Virginius Island exhibits, reflects the tendency to allow preservation goals to define the nature and scope of interpretation. Once again a physical structure, in this case a "fort," functions as the subject of an exhibit, giving visitors a historical chronology of its various displacements. While the fort is the subject of this exhibit, it is not an agent responsible in any way for its movements, and we are given no reasons for its being dismantled and vandalized other than its "fame" as John Brown's stronghold. Adjectives used to describe the building's movements also help personify the fort, as if it actually seemed unsettled and victimized by forced emigration from its natural "birthplace" in Harpers Ferry. "Dismantled" in 1891 and later "rescued" in 1895, the hapless fort's volatile history finally abates in 1968 when the Park Service safely returns it to its original location. In this description, the Park Service has provided the fort with an agency it did not possess, thereby endowing upon itself the role of heroic preservationist for bringing the fort back to its rightful birthplace.

The Park Service's tendency to personify material structures also displaces an emphasis on human history. Harpers Ferry's local citizens, for example, ironically suffered a similar fate to that of the fort: the residents were continuously uprooted and displaced—and their lives sometimes destroyed—by a spate of natural and human disasters in the late nineteenth and early twentieth centuries. Brown, too, is displaced by historic preservationist discourse, his complex legacy condensed to his occupation of the fort in 1859.

The fort's potential as a vehicle of symbolic action, whether for the promotion of larger debates about contemporary race relations, about the history of slavery in America, about the negotiation between sacred "natural" laws and secular "public" laws, or even about Brown himself, goes unfulfilled in this exhibit. The fort, whose popularity in American memory was once tied to meanings surrounding Brown's raid, is here described as coveted merely because of its fame. The fort as symbol, then, appears anesthetized in this exhibit, rendered a souvenir devoid of meaning rather than as a vessel of much larger significance.

There are ways, however, that the NPS can demonstrate how the preservation of a building affects human lives. For example, the fort's "movements" over the years could be explained by the needs of different groups to use the fort as a symbol or memorial to support a particular cause or idea. Storer College, for example, an all-black college located a few miles north of downtown Harpers Ferry, brought the fort to the campus in 1909 so it could serve as an inspirational physical symbol of black emancipation. Storer inscribed the following memorial to Brown on the fort's façade in 1918, which is still plainly visible to HFNHP visitors:

That this nation might have a new birth of freedom.
That slavery should be removed forever from American soil.
JOHN BROWN
And his 21 men gave their
Lives
To commemorate their
Heroism this tablet is

Placed on this building
Which has since been
Known as
JOHN BROWN'S FORT
By the
Alumni of Storer College
1918

Brown's fort, in this memorial, functions as a symbol of heroic sacrifice for the cause of black freedom. The plaque and the Park Service's
"John Brown's Fort" interpretive marker both stress the themes of birth,
tragedy, and a renewal made possible through heroic sacrifice. The Storer
memorial treats these themes more explicitly of course, as it pays tribute to Brown and his raiders' sacrifices, while the NPS's heroic preservationist role in "John Brown's Fort" is implied through its characterization of the fort's tumultuous "movements" preceding its return to
Harpers Ferry. Sharp contrasts also are evident in how the two artifacts
use the past as a motive for present and future change. The Storer memorial connects Brown's raid to the ongoing, abstract pursuit of "black
freedom," avoiding the more finite language of "black emancipation,"
which would have suggested that Brown and his raiders' sacrifices had
been redeemed through the Fourteenth Amendment.

Conversely, by ending its exhibit with a brief description of the fort's
rightful 1968 return to its near original location, the Park Service's interpretive marker keeps its subject rooted in the past, making it difficult for
visitors to discern the relevance of the fort to contemporary public life.

Storer's plaque can also be read as a fragment of a larger emancipationist memory. The popular origins of the emancipation vision and its
emphasis on national rebirth through a renewed commitment to racial
equality are commonly tied to Lincoln's Gettysburg Address, a more sanitized route for African Americans to secure mainstream approval for
what was then a radical cause. The first two lines of the Storer plaque are
therefore very typical, borrowing directly from Lincoln's address the key
passages that encouraged a rebirth of racial equality.

The emancipationist memory is absent from the Park Service interpretive markers created during the late 1960s at Harpers Ferry, which is
surprising given the relevance of racial equality themes in the broader

national context of racial riots and civil rights legislation. This pattern would change, however, and the fragment of emancipationist memory reflected in Storer College's plaque dedicated to John Brown would get resurrected in other exhibits in the park, specifically those created by the Park Service in the mid-1990s.

Emancipationist Memory and the John Brown Museum

Directly across the street from "Brown's fort" is the recently completed John Brown Museum, the largest interpretive area in the historical park and centrally located at the corner of Shenandoah and Potomac streets in Lower Town Harpers Ferry. Many of the themes in the museum's exhibits are repeated in other museums recently completed in Harpers Ferry, including the African-American History Museum and a small, single-room museum devoted to life in Harpers Ferry during the Civil War.[24] The museum is organized into three separate interpretive areas (three rooms, each with a different theme); each subsequent room implicitly shapes the meaning of the previous room(s). The museum is notable for its use of several different forms of interpretation, including film, photographs and drawings, interactive media, material artifacts, and narrative description. The style, form, and content of newer park exhibits differ dramatically from those of the older exhibits. John Brown Museum exhibits appear more open-ended and inquisitive, allowing visitors more room to generate answers for themselves while also being more aware of how the past can enlighten the present.

The museum's three-part structure begins by offering visitors more control over interpreting Brown but then constrains interpretations of his memory as visitors proceed through the museum's linear structure. The museum gradually imposes continuity on Brown's place in history by situating his raid within a master national narrative of inexorable liberty and equality made possible through an ongoing tradition of American protest. Although the museum's critique of the government's failure to protect the basic rights of its citizens in the second room of the museum is surprising, animosity and bitterness toward the government are not interpretations the NPS wants its visitors to take from their museum experience. Rather, the third and final room of the museum, which contextualizes Brown's raid within a history of democratic protest, gleans a sense of hopefulness from the individuals and groups who have taken advantage of their right to express themselves freely and protest peacefully. This emphasis on citizen "rights" rather than "duties" is a striking departure from a tradition of encouraging duty to country, or what Edward Linenthal calls "patriotic veneration."[25]

The exhibits in the recently opened museum are notable for their allegiance to the emancipationist memory of the Civil War that had been expressed by black leaders such as Frederick Douglass and W.E.B. DuBois after the war and eventually were overshadowed by reunion sentiments in the 1880s. The museum, therefore, challenges the reconciliationist memory dominant not only in the broader Civil War culture but also contained in many other NPS Civil War sites, especially battlefields.

Part 1 of the John Brown Museum: The Many Images of John Brown

Judging by the exhibits displayed in the foyer of the John Brown Museum, interpretation has been wrested loose from preservation, as these recent exhibits tend not to depend as much on salvaged material objects to tell the park's story. Immediately upon entering the museum visitors are faced with an open-ended question rather than a declarative statement of fact. Brown biographer Stephen Vincent Benet's quote "You can weigh John Brown's body well enough, but how and in what balance weigh John Brown?" greets visitors, boldly challenging them to assess Brown's ambiguous legacy. The openness of interpretive exhibits in the museum also seems apparent in the adjoining wall exhibit titled "Perspectives," which allows supporters and detractors of Brown to use their own words to evaluate him:

PERSPECTIVES
I go joyfully, in behalf of millions that "have no rights" that this great and glorious, this Christian Republic, "is bound to respect."
—John Brown, November 1859

All Virginia . . . should stand forth as one man and say to fanaticism . . . whenever you advance a hostile foot upon our soil, we will welcome you with bloody hands and hospitable graves.
—James L. Kemper, Delegate to the
Virginia General Assembly, 1859

It was [John Brown's] peculiar doctrine that man has a perfect right to interfere by force with the slaveholder, in order to rescue the slaves. I agree with him.

—Henry David Thoreau, October 30, 1859

If John Brown did not end the war that ended slavery, he did at least begin the war that ended slavery.

—Frederick Douglass, May 30, 1881

The heading for this exhibit demonstrates a shift in the Park Service's tendency toward literal interpretations of the past. By acknowledging the existence of competing "perspectives," the NPS demonstrates an awareness of how point of view can alter understandings of history. The "perspectives" are not too divergent, however, as three of the four represent the abolitionist perspective, and all three abolitionists hold a higher place than Kemper in public memory generally. The abolitionist support of Brown is also portrayed here as unified, despite the allegations made by some abolitionists immediately following the raid of Brown's irrational and misguided use of force. Statements supporting Brown and his cause are sandwiched between Kemper's inflammatory statement, diminishing the once commonly held perception of Brown's radicalism and supplanting it with Kemper's wild threat of greeting unwelcome outsiders with "bloody hands and hospitable graves."

Brown defends his cause and Thoreau affirms it while Douglass, twenty-one years removed from the raid, is able to frame Brown as the inspiration for the Civil War. Douglass, by having the final word, so to speak, is able to foreground the issue of slavery as the cause of the war, helping naturalize emancipation as the war's most important legacy, something he was unable to do in his own lifetime. The emancipationist memory of the war had lost momentum by the late 1870s, argues David Blight, as many had grown weary of years of partisan bickering over Reconstruction politics, preferring instead the reassuring sentimentalism of sectional reunification.[26]

Additional hints of the Park Service's use of the emancipationist memory are evident in an illustrated summary of Brown's raid, located adjacent to the "Perspectives" exhibit, with each illustration supported by the following captions:

1. John Brown's concern for four million enslaved African-Americans prompted him to take action.
2. Local militia engaged John Brown and his raiders on the grounds of the U.S. Armory.
3. U.S. Marines stormed the fire engine house of the U.S. Armory, where Brown and his men were hiding out.
4. The storming party of Marines wounded and seized Brown. Ten of Brown's men died during the raid.
5. Within two weeks of the raid, a Virginia court convicted Brown of murder, treason, and inciting slave rebellion.
6. John Brown sat on his own coffin en route to the gallows on December 2, 1859.
7. Fifteen hundred soldiers surrounded the site of Brown's execution.
8. The Civil War began 18 months after John Brown seized the federal armory in Harpers Ferry.

This seemingly straightforward chronological account of Brown's raid and trial situates Brown and his men as passive agents "acted upon" by the "storming party" of Marines. In fact, the narrative omits altogether Brown's seizure of federal property, substituting a description of his initial attack with a summary of his justification for the raid. By emphasizing Brown's purpose rather than the means used to carry out the raid, the exhibit encourages visitors to dwell upon the philosophy behind the raid rather than the violent actions taken by Brown and his men during the raid itself. The Marines, as active agents, appear to take the offensive role, initially "engaging" Brown, then "storming" the firehouse, and eventually "wounding" and "killing" Brown's men as well as "seizing" Brown, displacing attention on the raiders' initial seizure of the arsenal and their taking of hostages.

An emancipationist memory of the Civil War's legacy also appears to be used to temporally frame the "origins" and effects of Brown's raid. The first and last captions once again neatly frame slavery as the cause of the war, implying in turn the centrality of emancipation as the war's greatest legacy and positioning Brown as catalyst for black liberation. By logical deduction, then, the description invites visitors to "fill in" the conclusion that the war, provoked by disagreements over the rights of four million enslaved African Americans, resulted in their emancipation.

The identification of slavery as the war's primary cause and emancipation as its primary outcome were interpretations of the war promoted by abolitionists such as Douglass, who hoped these arguments would eventually function as unquestioned assumptions to ground Reconstruction policy. By contrast, in the nineteenth century, states' rights, Southern "honor," conflicting regional economies, preservation of the Union—and, as was commonplace during the time of reconciliation, a general ignorance of the war's causes altogether—all would have been more likely to be cited than slavery as causes of the war.[27]

The NPS's use of the emancipationist memory becomes more explicit when their newer exhibits are compared to older, closely related exhibits discussed earlier, such as this brief description of Brown's raid, written in 1968, and located in front of the arsenal as part of the "John Brown's Fort" interpretive marker: "On October 16, 1859, the abolitionist John Brown and his men attacked Harpers Ferry. By the following afternoon the local militia had penned the raiders in this building. United States Marines stormed the building at dawn on the 18th and captured Brown. Convicted of murder, treason, and inciting slaves to rebellion, he was hanged in nearby Charles Town on December 2, 1859."

Although many of the factual details contained in the two summaries are similar, the older exhibit, unlike the more recent one, does not situate slavery, Brown, and the Civil War within a broader trajectory of racial progress. Rather, the marker once again uses a building to serve as the context for a mimetic interpretation of a past event. Furthermore, temporal boundaries are clearly demarcated in the 1968 exhibit, citing Brown's raid as a point of origin and his execution as the end of the brief narrative.

Part 2 of the John Brown Museum: Slavery in Nineteenth-Century America

The second room of the John Brown Museum subtly justifies Brown's raid by contextualizing it within the oppressive history of slavery, especially in the antebellum period. A "slavery time line" faces visitors on the far wall across the entrance to the second room, chronicling the institution's nearly three-century existence in the United States. Potentially inflammatory quotes from Brown frame the two doorways leading to the third room. These quotes boldly indict the hypocrisy of American institutions that supported freedom but protected the legality of slavery, while excerpts from Theodore Weld's abolitionist tract *American Slavery as It Is* form the basis for an exhibit on the inhumane treatment of slaves. Many of the themes in this room are repeated and elaborated upon in the African-American History Museum located on High Street in the Lower Town section of Harpers Ferry.

The exhibits in this room, taken as a whole, are consistent with emancipationist memory, but by no means does this perspective reflect a consensual black memory of the war. Prominent black Southerners like Booker T. Washington, for example, wanted to supplant painful memories of slavery with the cooperative images of racial peace manifested by black contributions to economic growth. Washington's version of the war was essentially reconciliationist; he argued in the 1890s that blacks and whites were both disenfranchised economically at the end of the war and could mutually benefit by black contributions to industry.[28] Washington's rhetoric was appealing to Southern whites because it made few demands for federal intervention on behalf of African Americans, upheld social segregation between the races, and reinforced the subordinate position of blacks by citing misguided Reconstruction policies that prematurely propelled blacks up the economic and political hierarchy. This strand of reconciliationist memory shared the tendency toward historical forgetfulness, preferring to forsake past allegations of wrongdoing and orient perceptions toward "black progress."

The Park Service's support of emancipationist memory, rather than Washington's version of reconciliationist memory, is evidenced in an exhibit in the African-American History museum—located across the street from the John Brown Museum—titled "Clash of the Titans: DuBois versus Washington." A biographical snapshot of each leader is followed by a summary of their differing views on black empowerment. A subheading titled "The Clash" contrasts their positions: "W.E.B. DuBois disagreed strongly with Booker T. Washington's position on civil rights. He felt that Washington's so-called 'accommodationist policies' undermined the quest for equality. DuBois organized the Niagara Movement to demand equal enforcement of the law for all races and active political involvement at all levels of society." In this exhibit visitors get to react to Washington's policies from DuBois's point of view, which has been the subject of many exhibits dealing with early twentieth-century civil rights. The African-American History Museum, in particular, with its repeated mention of the Niagara Movement's ties to Storer College and Harpers Ferry, implies that Washington's views are extraneous to the cause of black equality and would only slow the momentum of what, with hindsight, is now considered the correct course of social change.

Emancipationists like DuBois, while sharing aspects of Washington's version of a reconciliationist memory, diverged from Washington by insisting upon recognizing emancipation and the subsequent Union victory as decisive first steps in the legal and social enfranchisement of blacks. Advocates of emancipationist memory were also less likely to concede that slaves' African background rendered them inferior to whites; DuBois, for example, went to great lengths to idealize African culture, prefiguring the larger twentieth-century Afrocentric movement. At the same time, emancipationists were careful to describe slavery's oppressive effects on black life without undercutting blacks' potential as equals. Conversely, reconciliationists like Washington were more apt to downplay the detrimental effects of slavery by arguing that slaves' African background had left blacks morally and intellectually bereft to begin with, and slavery, while an unjust institution, had actually improved their lot. He argued in 1903, "When the Negro went into slavery he was without anything which might be properly called a language; when he came out of slavery he was able to speak the English tongue . . . when he entered slavery he had little working knowledge of agriculture, mechanics, or household duties; when he emerged . . . he was almost the entire dependence in a large section of our country for agricultural, mechanical and domestic labor."[29]

Washington's accommodationist policies, when judged from the perspective of diversity consciousness of the late 1990s, appear inattentive toward black equality. In truth, Washington's more pragmatic approach to race relations helped secure moderate economic gains for blacks and inspired many to achieve through self-reliance what could not be acquired through federal policies that abandoned Reconstruction. Washington was popular among blacks for the same reasons that led many to interpret Brown's raid as a failure; many measured progress in practical terms, not through idealistic musings. Conversely, DuBois's idealism, combined with his leadership inexperience, contributed to the Niagara Movement's short and uneventful tenure. Yet that same idealism, while impractical by nineteenth-century standards, can resonate more clearly in a day and age when most are interested in maintaining at least the appearance of tolerance toward diversity, a position that requires inspiring voices from the past to legitimate the inevitability of that ideal.

An additional perspective on black memory of the war also emerged in less secular circles in the nineteenth century. Influential ministers such as Henry McNeal Turner saw slavery and emancipation as signs of providential influence, believing that emancipation, rather than serving as new point of origin for black equality in America, was a major turning point in God's plan to return freedmen to Africa and secure its redemption. Many black Christian theologians believed that God, not politics, the law, or economics, would liberate black Americans. Ultimately, black millennialists interpreted emancipation as one event in a protracted, God-ordained plan to rescue a more holy Christianity from corrupt Anglo-Saxon Christians.[30]

Exhibits devoted to slavery in the John Brown Museum are inspired more by the emancipationist memory advocated by the likes of Douglass and DuBois than by black memories of the war fashioned from reconciliationist and millennialist perspectives. The exhibits in this room challenge visitors to imagine the social, political, economic, and moral dilemmas posed by slavery in the nineteenth century. Contrary to the "black progress" rhetoric of African American millennialists and reconciliationists, the exhibits dwell on the tragedies and horrors of slavery, including newspaper ads from slaves and ex-slaves searching for family members lost in the internal slave trade.

Resistance is another theme of slavery exhibits. Nat Turner's slave rebellion is summarized somewhat sympathetically in a brief exhibit on resistance; some African Americans killed in retaliation to Turner's rebellion are labeled "innocents" while Turner's victims are not. Also included in this exhibit are short descriptions of the 1839 slave revolt aboard the ship *Amistad* and a failed attack by slaves on Richmond in 1800. These exhibits also reflect a tendency in emancipationist memory to draw parallels between the colonists' quest for liberty from British rule and blacks' quest for liberty from the legal institution of slavery. "I have nothing more to offer than what George Washington would have had to offer," begins a quote from one of the Richmond insurgents prior to his hanging, "had he been taken by the British and put on trial by them. I have adventured my life in endeavoring to obtain the liberty of my countrymen, and am a willing sacrifice to their cause." Selective quotations such as this make it clear that the Park Service encourages visitors to see black and colonist resistance as analogous. This point is made explicit in an exhibit titled "Protests in Democracy" located in the third and final room of the John Brown Museum.

Part 3 of the John Brown Museum: Brown's Twentieth-Century Legacy

The "Protests in Democracy" exhibit begins by contextualizing Brown's raid within a history of American protest:

> A Tradition of Protest
> John Brown's raid in 1859, although unusual for its attack on a federal installation, is part of a long tradition of protest and dissent in America. The U.S. was born in protest. In the years before the American Revolution, colonists repeatedly and passionately spoke out against the laws and policies of England. Essentially, they rebelled with violence and war.

Brown's attack, despite its "unusual" character, nevertheless exists comfortably alongside the American Revolution as a form of protest. The favorable analogy enables Brown's raid to share the legitimacy of the American Revolution as a protest movement, not to mention its mythic force as a birthing of American freedom. The analogy also facilitates a seamless continuity in the country's master narrative of freedom, clearing a logical space for the classification of emancipation as the country's "Second American Revolution," which has been a common rhetorical feature of emancipationists' narrative reframing of the past.

History also seems less deterministic and more subject to the whims of human choices in these exhibits. The exhibit "Am I Not a Man? Am I Not a Woman?" for example, describes how slaves were viewed and treated as material property that could be purchased, sold, and exchanged:

> Slaves were valued both as personal property and for the work they performed. By definition of the law, slaves were a commodity that could be bought, sold, inherited, managed and "hired out" for the owner's profit. Although legally defined as property, slaves were people. Potential and actual economic transactions affected the lives of African-Americans dramatically.

Ironically, the exhibit describes a process of dehumanization not unlike the form of earlier HFNHP preservationist rhetoric found in exhibits that anthropomorphized material property. Here, however, the process is reversed; the Park Service explains how behavior toward others can be rationalized through language that equates people with material property. "Slavery" and "property," the exhibit seems to argue, once perceived as interdependent, can now be readily dislodged from one another, exposing a onetime literal relationship as the cruel and dehumanizing nomenclature that it is. Recent exhibits such as this make it easier for visitors to understand how people have used interpretation in the past to selectively create their social and political worlds. The relationship between slavery and property, the exhibit illustrates, is not natural; it is a social construction that legitimated a system of oppression and eased the guilt of those who practiced it.

The indeterminate course of history also seems apparent in an exhibit consisting of a series of questions that address the important moral, political, social, and economic quandaries of the antebellum era. "Are African slaves human beings, or are they a lower species?" begins a subheading on moral questions of the antebellum period. The exhibit continues: "Are blacks and whites equal? Should all blacks be returned to Africa? Does the bible support or condemn slavery? Can a good Christian be a slave holder? Does history justify slavery?" These questions not only give visitors more control over the interpretive process but also make the past appear amenable to change based on human choices and actions, including the role of interpretation in creating the answers to these important questions, which then function as assumptions that ground public policy.

Exhibits interpreting slavery are also especially critical of federal laws that allowed slavery to legally exist. The NPS uses several quotations from Brown hanging over prominent spots in the room to make their constitutional argument:

All of the national acts (which apply to slavery) are false, to the words, spirit, and intention of the Constitution of the United States and the Declaration of Independence.
—John Brown, 1858

I believe in the Golden Rule and the Declaration of Independence. I think they both mean the same thing; and it is better that a whole generation should perish off the face of the earth—men, women, and children die by a violent death than one lot of either should live in this country.

—John Brown, 1859

Brown, the onetime radical abolitionist, is here the reasonable constitutionalist opining about the hypocrisy of federal laws. Criticisms of slavery are not uncommon in contemporary U.S. culture, of course. However, the Park Service, which has utilized the reconciliationist memory at many of its other Civil War sites, has generally avoided interpreting issues of slavery and racial tension. The appropriation of the emancipationist memory, then, forces the Park Service, as the government's official voice of its past, to critique its own complicity in maintaining racial oppression. Within the context of a dominant reconciliationist memory of the war, then, the slavery exhibits function to "de-mythologize" the ignored or often sentimentalized picture of slavery represented through a reconciliationist lens.

The museum's critique of the federal government is, for the most part, softened considerably in this third and final room of the John Brown Museum, which seamlessly connects Brown's raid to other forms of twentieth-century protest. The room's exhibits limit the criticism of federal laws and institutions to the distant past and attempt to restore its visitors' faith in America's legal and political doctrines and institutions. If the museum's second room "de-mythologizes" slavery from its sentimentalized reconciliationist memory, then the "conclusion" to the museum, by draping its walls with American flags and photographs of former presidents Jefferson and Washington, "re-mythologizes" the emancipationist memory by using it to make the country's past seem predestined and heroic.

Visual symbols are important sources of meaning in this room. The widespread use of American flags, the colors red, white, and blue to frame the border of exhibits, and pictures of ex-presidents whose impact is not relevant to the exhibits' themes suggests that visual iconography invites visitors to apply a more mythological frame to interpret Brown's contemporary meanings. Pictures of Washington and Jefferson, in particular, would appear to function as emotional patriotic triggers of memory as visitors complete their trip through the museum. These pictures simplify the active process of interpretation from the preceding room's exhibits and replace it with a more instantly recognizable and passive mythic frame of meaning.

Collectively, the exhibits in this room would appear to strike a reassuring and optimistic tone and in the process restore a more deterministic trajectory to the course of history and memory. One of the most prominent exhibits in this room, "African-Americans on Brown," is devoted to interpreting John Brown's lasting legacy and appropriates aspects of emancipationist memory to interpret Brown's legacy as inspiring people to utilize their basic rights to promote social and political change.

"African-Americans on Brown" includes a collage of quotations from prominent nineteenth- and early twentieth-century black leaders and several short descriptions of Brown's lingering impact in Harpers Ferry. The descriptions include the frequently cited pilgrimage by the Women's Colored League to the Alexander Murphy farm in 1896 and the Niagara Movement's meeting in Harpers Ferry in 1906. The exhibit's featured quotations are from Douglass and DuBois, the two most prominent hero figures (besides Brown) represented in the park's newer exhibits, including the two museums devoted to African American history. Douglass, the most vocal nineteenth-century advocate of an emancipationist memory of the Civil War, is quoted from a memorial address he gave in Brown's honor at Storer College in Harpers Ferry in 1881, one of several quotes from this speech featured throughout the park: "Until this blow was struck, the prospect for freedom was dim, shadowy, and uncertain. The irrepressible conflict was one of words, votes, and compromises. When John Brown stretched forth his arm the sky was cleared. The time for compromise was gone—the armed hosts of freedom stood face to face over the chasm of a broken Union—and the clash of arms was at hand.—May 30, 1881."

Douglass's speech seems meaningful as a way to bracket Brown's raid as the war narrative's point of origin, especially in the context of the park's other recent exhibits as well as a country one hundred and thirty years removed from the speech. As a result, African American freedom is naturalized as the cause of, inspiration for, and consequence of the war, thereby enabling a broadened revision of the country's master narrative of inexorable progress toward freedom and equality.

Douglass used this speech in 1881 as a strategic response to the exigen-

cies posed by the fading promises of Reconstruction and the tranquiliz-
ing effects of a country in the sentimental throes of white sectional reunion. Although changing his audience's basic assumptions about the war's
underlying meanings might have been a focus of his speech, Douglass's
goals were also very immediate and specific. His struggle was against the
complacency of Civil War memory and the desire among many for sectional compromise, materialized through the symbolic gestures of for-
giveness by former veterans' handshakes across the "bloody chasms" of
war. Douglass tries desperately to reverse the meaning of the dominant
words and images of complacent reconciliationist memory, rendering
"compromise" a pejorative term and identifying the bloody "chasm"
as a point of former physical confrontation rather than white intraracial
harmony. Visitors, over one hundred years removed from these debates,
would probably be less inclined to respond to the great sense of urgency
created in Douglass's speech, given that active conflict over Civil War
memory has, with some notable exceptions, abated in recent years.[31]

The Park Service's use of emancipationist memory in the 1990s helps
visitors manage fundamental, commonsense meanings about the country's basic identity and purpose. The NPS's representation of Douglass's
and DuBois's words is inspiring today because their rhetoric resonates
with the diffused myth of national progress toward equality, not because they help visitors understand the challenges of contemporary inequality. In these exhibits, the absence of contemporary voices of black
memory as well as a lack of examples of specific modern forms of racial
inequality render such racial struggles a part of the past. The Park Service, of course, is not obliged to raise awareness about the current ob-
stacles to racial progress. Despite the fact that they are invited to leave
the museum with a sense of satisfaction and complacency about current
black-white relations, visitors need to recognize that the struggle for racial progress is always ongoing and continuous.

Conclusion

The inclusion of an African American perspective on Harpers Ferry's
past has brought the Park Service closer to constructing a relativistic
history of the site—a stark contrast to their traditionally "objectivist"
approach toward history that has been propped up by the practice of

historic preservation. The incorporation of emancipationist voices into Civil War memory is long overdue and welcome, especially within a Civil War culture that has privileged the memory of white reconciliation. In addition, by relying on African American memories rather than professional or academic histories to tell the story of racial progress, HFNHP interpretive exhibits are lively, provocative, and diffuse. Furthermore, those memories are also organized to serve the interests of a federal government perspective, which is accomplished by situating African American memories within a nationalistic narrative of continuing progress. The emancipationist memory, which links racial equality to the promises made in the Declaration of Independence and the Constitution, relies heavily on an interpretation of the Civil War as a cataclysmic and regenerative event that was necessary for the country to eradicate slavery and rededicate itself to "a new birth of freedom."

The emancipationist memory is based on keeping a selective memory of the war alive in the imaginations of the American public and policymakers. As a result of the Park Service's appropriation of the emancipationist legacy, then, memory becomes an active part of interpretation at Harpers Ferry. Conversely, the reconciliationist legacy and its ideology of white superiority, which were largely materialized through the veterans' reunions held on former Civil War battlefields, were modeled on a pattern of ignoring or forgetting the causes and consequences of the war. Thus it is not surprising that NPS Civil War battlefields have tended to "preserve" the memory of reconciliation, unwittingly perpetuating a legacy of the war as a battle fought with equal valor by white soldiers of both sides, largely through creating inscrutably detailed, depoliticized interpretations of the battles themselves.

By incorporating voices of memory into its recent interpretive exhibits, the NPS has made Harpers Ferry National Historical Park a more stimulating and provocative place to visit. Although its recent exhibits challenge the style and themes of earlier exhibits overdetermined by a preservationist orientation, the Park Service still makes the past seem distant and remotely connected to the present. This is, of course, the heart and soul of the parks' popularity. The parks owe much of their appeal to the feelings of nostalgia and escapism from modern life that is created through building preservation and natural beautification. Yet when judged as works of memory designed to help expose and alleviate the root causes of racism and prejudice in the mid-1990s period of American culture in which they were written, the exhibits seem ideologically obsolete.

By relying almost exclusively on voices of black memory whose wishes for basic civil rights appear by today's standards to have been granted by the Civil Rights acts of the 1960s, Harpers Ferry's exhibits leave visitors with the impression that racial inequality is a thing of the past. It appears that historically marginalized memories are deemed fit for inclusion into dominant, "official" memory only when their radicalism can be tamed over time, forcing African American memories to play a never-ending game of "catch-up" with the present, leaving those memories—and progressive social change itself—perpetually one step behind. The Park Service's emphasis on citizen "rights" rather than "duties" is laudable, although time will tell if they are able to make visitors feel disturbed, rather than mildly complacent, about their past and unsettled, rather than pacified, about its unresolved legacies.

II
Violence and Memory

3
Savage and Heroic War Memories at Gettysburg National Military Park

For over a century dominant public memory of the battle of Gettysburg has helped Americans imagine a battle full of resplendent drama and climactic narrative tension. Over time many have come to view the battle as a glorious struggle that foreshadowed ultimate Union victory and featured countless acts of valor, especially those performed by Confederates during the fateful Pickett's Charge.[1] For many contemporaries, the "High Water Mark" of the Confederacy signifies the end of the war, or at least the beginning of the end.[2] But for many of the soldiers at Gettysburg, the battle signified the beginning of a war of attrition that would alter how they fought, experienced, and remembered the war.

The battle of Gettysburg occupies a liminal space or "turning point" between two interpretations of the experience of war articulated by the soldiers who fought it. "Courage's war," as Gerald F. Linderman explains, was essentially a materialization of the era's dominant heroic masculine ideology that guided Union and Confederate soldiers' expectations and early experiences of the war. Courage, exemplified by calm resolve under the most fearful battle circumstances, was the ultimate test of one's manliness and was achieved through strong faith, self-control, and an unbending commitment to duty. Adherence to these principles, it was widely believed, would yield victory, honor, and immortality.

As the war dragged on, however, the old system of values increasingly failed to match soldiers' experiences, and disillusionment began to spread through the ranks of both armies. The recurrent and devastating failure of frontal assaults, and offensive strategy generally, forced earlier heroic images of the charge to coexist with despondent accounts of their futility and desperation. Religious faith, its ardent supporters believed, would dispel fear, offer divine protection, and procure victory, although the reality of depersonalized mass warfare would erode, for many, such convictions. Not only was early belief in the decisiveness of individual will and courage in battle shaken by the magnitude of destruction wrought by the grapeshot and canister of long-range artillery, but individual agency itself was stripped of its power by autonomous machinery in the terrifying and desolate trench warfare of 1864–65.

Civil War soldiers' largely heroic constructions of war, then, gradually yielded to a more savage and brutal war experience. But at the time of Gettysburg, the gulf between the savage and heroic was less distinguishable. The experience of Gettysburg, with its combination of dramatic frontal assaults and flanking maneuvers and massive attrition, could especially reduce the binary between savagery and heroism to a fluid interplay—what some observers could see as the war's most glorious site of valor in the Confederates' final, courageous charge across Seminary Ridge, for example, others could just as easily interpret as an unprecedented march of death.

The public memory of the battle of Gettysburg has not, however, sustained this dialectic. As an important symbol of America's patriotic heritage, heroic Gettysburg memory trumped its gloomy antithesis once and for all during the period of reconciliation in the late nineteenth century. In the following two chapters I resurrect the interplay between savage and heroic interpretations of the battle in order to create what I argue is an important space for a reading of the American Civil War as savage. As several scholars have recently demonstrated, extensive public commemoration of battles such as Gettysburg promoted a collective amnesia about the war's deeper causes and legacies, especially slavery. In these chapters, however, I explore forgetfulness of a different sort. Specifically, I argue that reconciliationist memory not only restored racial hegemony but also enabled prewar masculinity to regain its cultural dominance by repressing the war's grisly and savage post-Gettysburg years and with it their potentially transforming critique of heroic masculinity. I utilize, as a heuristic, the National Park Service's verbal and visual representations of combat at Gettysburg National Military Park (GNMP), a primary source of Gettysburg memory familiar to many Americans, to accomplish this objective.

This chapter begins with an examination of dominant constructions of masculinity that shaped many soldiers' interpretations of their initial war experience and explains how the war's devastation gradually challenged the cultural standard of manliness that existed at the beginning of the war. Then, using the first several wayside exhibits along the popular self-guided auto tour of the battlefield as a representative sample of verbal discourse, I identify and describe six interrelated ways that GNMP exhibits use the genre of military strategy writing to sublimate the centrality of battlefield injuring and killing, thereby helping to sustain a heroic interpretation of the battle of Gettysburg. I continue on the self-guided auto tour of the battlefield in chapter 4, this time demonstrating how the visual rhetoric of the physical landscape, monuments, and Civil War photographs restores the ideology of heroic white masculinity to its prewar hegemony by contextualizing combat within a vast, bucolic, and serene rural space. Overall, I conclude in these two chapters that even though the Park Service helps institutionalize a heroic interpretation of the battle, brutal and savage readings of Gettysburg exist just beneath its surface.

But why, some might reasonably ask, reintroduce a savage interpretation of the battle of Gettysburg when the battle's memory has served such an inspirational and patriotic national purpose? As the "beginning of the end" of the Civil War narrative, dominant battle of Gettysburg memory makes the war's final two bitter years seem anticlimactic and largely irrelevant. Rhetorically, a dominant heroic battle of Gettysburg memory restores the integrity and power of that heroic frame for the war as a whole, effectively sublimating to the margins the alternate savage narrative of the war most forcefully and patently represented in the experience and interpretation of "total warfare" in 1864–65.

A savage interpretation of Gettysburg, then, would reverse the battle's place in the war's overall temporal structure in public memory. Within the heroic frame the battle functions as the war's climactic conclusion, while the savage frame marks it as the beginning of a downward spiral of attrition that would foreshadow the total wars of the twentieth century. A savage public memory of Gettysburg could, then, productively critique prewar masculine ideology and its contributions to glorifying war as a rite of passage into manhood.

Furthermore, by exploring the relationship between the heroic and savage experience of the Civil War, this analysis can help expose a schism between civilian and military interpretations of the morality of the

Civil War. The Park Service utilizes the seemingly objective genre of military strategy discourse to create a heroic interpretation of the battle of Gettysburg, which, I contend, helps keep afloat civilian memories of war as a moral activity. Ironically, however, the ideology of masculinity, with its emphasis on honorable and civilized combat, helped create a heroic interpretation of war that largely undermined effective war strategy. As generals such as Jackson, Grant, and Sherman clearly understood, in war one side forces the other side to surrender by killing as many of its soldiers as possible, and it helps when you have soldiers who possess an indiscriminate, amoral, and "savage" attitude toward killing. The Park Service, then, is in a difficult position. Should they act as moralists and create a public memory of Civil War violence as morally just? Or, if they prioritize their role as military historians, do they help visitors directly confront the "effectiveness" of savagery as a military strategy?

Before examining the Park Service's interpretations of combat at Gettysburg, I outline the contours of Civil War soldiers' heroic and savage interpretations of their war experiences and how they reinforced and challenged the dominant masculine ideology of the Civil War era.

Heroic and Savage Interpretations of Civil War Combat

The individual Civil War soldier often was motivated to enlist and remain in the war for more personal and social reasons than the abstract political causes of states' rights or preservation of the Union espoused by politicians of the South and the North. Perhaps the most persuasive factor that influenced soldiers' fighting mentality and behavior was the cultural standard of manliness whose barometer became the battlefield in 1861. Much of the following account of soldiers' experience of combat is indebted to Gerald F. Linderman's *Embattled Courage: The Experience of Combat in the American Civil War,* one of the most preeminent scholarly studies of the Civil War soldier experience.

The Courageous or Heroic War

"Courage," writes Linderman, "had for Civil War soldiers a narrow, rigid, and powerful meaning: heroic action undertaken without fear."[3] The most tangible and admired expressions of courage were demonstrated by those who remained stoic and composed under the most tense and chaotic conditions of battle. Watching his fellow Confederates scatter following a Union artillery shelling, one observer noted that the spectacle of seeing General Turner Ashby react as if the barrage hadn't occurred made him appear "totally indifferent to the hellish fire raining all about him."[4] Civil War archetypes of courage J.E.B. Stuart and Thomas "Stonewall" Jackson, who also personified for many of their soldiers the era's other idealized masculine traits of godliness, honor, and knightliness, were revered for their "utter disregard for danger" in the face of utmost peril.

Modeling courage of this type required, many soldiers believed, the highest powers of self-control. Fear was widely seen as a form of weakness and cowardice, and it, along with courage, was most evident during the charge, which was the supreme trial of manliness. "In the first years of the war," Linderman writes, "the rank-and-file held themselves to a strict standard, that of fighting 'man fashion.' They were expected to wait stoically through the tense and difficult period just prior to battle; to stand and receive enemy fire without replying to it; and to resist all urges to quicken their pace under fire, to dodge or duck shells, or to seek cover."[5] Cowardliness, the opposite of courage, was therefore invoked to describe those who ducked, ran, darted, or dove to the ground.

Manliness, Linderman observes, was often used interchangeably with courage. Quite simply, courageous behavior was perceived as masculine, and even the perfect fulfillment of masculinity, while acts of cowardice (that is, expressions of fear) were tagged as feminine. One Federal soldier bemoaned his actions at Antietam, remarking that it was the only battlefield that "I could not look at without being unmanned." Manliness was also closely linked to the notion of honor, which was a gentlemanly virtue defined by an amalgam of norms and behaviors, including keeping one's word, maintaining a dignified respect for the character of others, including opponents, magnanimity, and of course acts of courage. The connection between honor and courage was most evident in references to the "honorable wound" and "honorable death." One Federal soldier remarked early in the war that wounded soldiers taken from the battlefield to the field hospital were "as cheerful a lot of fellows . . . as you can imagine. Wounded men coming from under fire are, as a rule, cheerful, often jolly. Being able to get, honorably, from under fire, with the mark of manly service to show, is enough to make a fellow cheerful, even with a hole in him."[6] Honorable wounds, from this soldier's vantage, are sustained while exhibiting acts of individual courage, which in turn reinforce one's manliness.

Honor and death shared an unusual relationship by today's standards. Linderman and more recently Drew Gilpin Faust argue that soldiers were socialized to believe that it was better to die an honorable death on the battlefield than to bear the label of a coward. Having observed the dismissal of a New Jersey officer accused of cowardice, George Stevens wrote, "how much better it would have been to have fallen nobly on that field of battle, honored and lamented, than to live to be degraded and despised." "Death before dishonor" might not have been part of an individual's code of honor prior to the war, but the pressure to conform to such standards amid a large group of one's peers was often too much for soldiers to resist.

The high value placed on honor convinced many that they were fighting a "gentleman's" war. Of course, the bifurcation between "civilized" and "uncivilized" was used to create and justify various power inequities in the nineteenth century, and so killing, lest it be deemed "uncivilized," had to be undertaken in ways that upheld the moral standards of the time period as defined by those in positions of power. One hallmark of "civilized" behavior was a pious Christian faith, which many soldiers believed would endow them with the strength necessary to act courageously, behave honorably, and come away from battle victorious. The prototypical Christian warriors were Generals Thomas "Stonewall" Jackson, Robert E. Lee, and J.E.B. Stuart. The causal relationship between godliness and courage was perceptible in soldiers' reactions to these men, whose calmness under intense conditions seemed to demonstrate the depths of their faith, and was widely emulated.

By placing their fate in the hands of the Almighty, soldiers believed they could gain some measure of control over their own fears and be protected from harm. It was not uncommon to hear stories repeated in Northern and Southern presses about the good fortune bestowed upon the faithful in battle, whether it be tales of the Bible that stopped a bullet from penetrating its owner's flesh or the "unseen hand" that protected the devoted from harm during intense forays into battle. Battlefield victory was also widely perceived early in the war to be conferred upon the most collectively faithful army. "When at the battle of Stone's River," Linderman writes, "Federal troops realized that the Confederates had begun to retreat, a member of the 64th Ohio began to sing the Doxology: 'Praise God from whom all blessings flow' was taken up first by his comrades, then by the regiment, and then ran up and down the line."[7]

A sense of duty also exerted a strong influence at the time, but its exact source and definition were amorphous and varied widely among soldiers. Duty was not subsumed as much by nationalism as it is today, and although state sovereignty and preservation of the Union were causes that brought men from both sides to enlist, widespread individualism also meant that the source of duty could extend from God to family, comrade, regiment, or unit. Linderman argues that no matter the source of one's duty, its presence was felt equally among the ranks of the enlisted. Here, too, the definition of duty is closely aligned with other masculine virtues of the day, such that duty becomes a form of honor, while both are upheld by courage, which is itself sustained through faith.

Courage, manliness, honor, godliness, and duty. These values helped form a fairly coherent ideology that shaped how soldiers experienced and interpreted combat. Linderman argues that "courage" stands at the center of this value system; all other values are subservient to it. Yet this privileging of behavior as the source of identity obscures the connection between "courage" and gender and race, for certainly this value system prescribes an ideal standard of behavior not for all cultural members and groups (certainly not blacks or women) but for Anglo-Saxon males in particular. Gender and race sanction and unify these values more than anything, it seems, and only with both in place as prerequisites—as they were at the beginning of the war in both armies—can all be judged by the same standard of courageous behavior.

Idealized standards of white masculinity, furthermore, would be a likely source of collective identification and shared meaning in armies separated by local, state, ethnic, and class differences. Soldiers' diaries and letters reflect these values, especially in the first two years of the war, their explanatory force withstanding even the most gruesome experiences, including the suffering from injury and the omnipresence of death. Robert Stiles, a Confederate artillery captain, noted with awe how Stonewall Jackson greeted, unmoved, the sight of a line of Mississippians crushed by a head-level volley of Northern artillery, their foreheads "stained with ooze and the trickle of blood": "Not a muscle quivered," Stiles wrote. "[H]e was the ideal of concentration—imperturbable, resistless."[8]

The Savage War

Few soldiers argued at the time that the same behavior that would lead many to praise Jackson for his composed and stoic reaction to killing could also be interpreted as contributing to the numbing, depersonalization of war that enables it to exist and continue indefinitely. There were, however, many signs early in the war that the virtues of manliness might not be of service or even aptly rewarded in a war that confounded soldiers' expectations. Disease, the monotony of camp life, and the experience of witnessing injury and death proved not only unnerving but contradictory to the romanticized expectations of war soldiers brought with them from home.

Disease ravaged both sides during the war; the number of deaths resulting from disease outnumbered combat deaths almost two to one. The first wave of disease tended to affect men from rural areas who had not been exposed to as many diseases as children, such as smallpox and measles, compared to boys in urban settings. The second wave of disease was associated with poor camp conditions, which worsened over time. Dysentery, malaria, and diarrhea all caused high numbers of discharges and fatalities. But the deaths resulting from illness were also disconcerting because the heroic ideology of masculinity did not render gallant those who suffered from disease. Fearlessness could be exhibited by not showing outward signs of pain and suffering, of course, but many believed that those who contracted disease were too weak of will to resist it.

Encounters with death were certainly not uncommon in 1860, nor was the sight of blood, a regular part of the hunting and fishing expeditions so typical of rural life. Yet Civil War soldiers were still shocked by the arbitrariness, extent, and appearance of the wounded and dead. Confederate chaplain James Sheeran remarked that he saw "perhaps . . . the most revolting scene I had ever witnessed" at the battle of Chancellorsville: "Our line of battle extended over some eight miles and for that distance you see the dead bodies of the enemy lying in every direction, some with their heads shot off, some with their brains oozing out, some pierced through the head with musket balls, some with their noses shot away, some with their mouths smashed, some wounded in the neck, some with broken arms or legs, some shot through the breast and some cut in two with shells."[9] The sights and sounds of killing, despite their horror, could still sustain a heroic interpretation, but it was the power and range of the military technology of the time that did the most to erode the validity of heroic masculinity and the tactic that served as its proof: the frontal assault.

The Mexican War of 1846 featured the single-shot, muzzle-loading musket, the same one featured in the Civil War. Civil War generals had learned from that experience that the musket was time consuming to load and inaccurate from distances of one hundred or more yards, leading Ulysses Grant to remark that one could be fired upon all day from a distance of a few hundred yards "without your finding it out."[10] The inaccuracy and inefficiency of the musket exalted the offensive minded—charging columns of soldiers who could withstand an initial volley of musket fire could often pounce upon the defenders before they could reload. The entire process was time consuming. After firing his weapon, a soldier would have to retrieve a cartridge from an encased wrapper that had to be opened with his teeth. Then, while holding the musket upright, the soldier would pour the gunpowder from the wrapper into the muzzle while separating out the cartridge, then insert the ball into the muzzle, tamp it in with a ramrod, and bring it to his waist to set a percussion cap on the nipple before bringing it to his shoulder. Linderman explains: "Civil War muzzle-loaders however were no longer smooth-bore but rifled—that is, their barrels were grooved in a way imparting to the bullet a spin that extended the weapon's effective range to distances between 300 and 400 yards. Charging columns could be brought under fire much earlier, at a half-mile's distance, and a much higher toll exacted. Even with the persistence of poor firing instruction and wretched firing discipline, rifling strengthened the hand of the defense decisively."[11]

Technological improvements even made it easier for soldiers to open rain-resistant paper cartridges. Despite the damage more efficient muskets caused, the technological changes did not alter offensive battle tactics overnight. Ranks of dead were arranged "as neatly as if on parade" at Antietam, while Federal soldier Thomas Galwey found bullets from Confederate muskets so intense that "almost every blade of grass is moving. . . . What we see now looks to us like systematic killing." The death tolls and strategic losses from frontal attacks were astounding. The attacks Grant ordered at Cold Harbor in the summer of 1864 resulted in 7,000 killed and wounded in less than an hour. Lee ordered approximately 12,000 soldiers to charge across Cemetery Ridge on the last day of the battle of Gettysburg, losing about half of those men. Confederate general John Bell Hood's willingness to go on the offensive cost him 10,000 troops at Decatur and 5,000 (against 600 Northern deaths) at Ezra Church.

By late 1863 and early 1864 strategy increasingly turned defensive, while offensive maneuvers began to incorporate more of the ducking and running that was perceived as so cowardly earlier in the war. The effectiveness of long-range musket fire also forced company officers determined to earn their soldiers' respect by calmly withstanding enemy fire to revise their habit. Linderman relays a story, for example, of officers of the 20th Massachusetts who ordered their men to the ground during an attack as they calmly strode around, only to lose two-thirds of their officers to death or injury. As the old values no longer seemed to be actualized in the gallant frontal assault and as soldiers learned to cope with the harsh realities of war by relying less on the heroic ideal and more on depersonalizing everything around them, new habits emerged. While earlier in the war it would have been common to refrain from shooting those enemies whose composure and steady resolve earned their opponents' honorable respect, those same officers were now seen as easy targets. Color-bearers, whose position at one time in the war was highly coveted, also became sought-after targets not only because they stood out so much but because it was believed that their task, which was to inspire a charge or rally for their regiment, would be undermined if whoever picked up the flag were shot.

Eventually both armies began to build earthworks to establish defenses to protect themselves from artillery and infantry attack. The change did not easily conform to the moral standards of heroic masculinity, especially for those who still abided by its norms. Hood was so against the works that Confederates who sought their protection "would imperil that spirit of devil-may-care independence and self-reliance which was one of their secret sources of power, and would, finally impair the morale of [the] Army." Hood felt that those who fought behind cover magnified their fears, as if the mounds of dirt themselves symbolized cowardice rather than protection. Yet the success of the earthworks forced those in combat to once again allow ideology to take a back seat to effective strategy. Fredericksburg was the first battle that the Confederates fought behind the earthworks, and their resounding victory led to its continued use. "As early as Gettysburg," writes Linderman, "it could be seen that the armies were so balanced in the quality of their arms and soldierly, if one were given the time to entrench, the other's assault would be almost sure to fail."[12]

While resigned to digging as part of the war's new strategy, soldiers could not fit their heroic ideology into its dreary, depersonalized reality. In what would be a foreshadowing of the terrible trench warfare on the Western front in World War I, soldiers from both sides dug in for months of continuous skirmishing, the onset of nighttime attacks, and increased use of sharpshooting. Complicated earthworks, especially at Petersburg, included trenches protected by abatis (felled trees) and chevaux-de-frise (sharpened stakes), giving battle a sense of permanence while increasing the distances separating combatants. In his seminal work on the psychology of enmity, Sam Keen writes that as distance between combatants widens, killing becomes easier, and combatants no longer have to confront one another as human beings but as abstractions.[13] Soldiers' experiences of trench warfare suggest that opponents separated by distance and covered behind earthworks made killing easier psychologically. Sharpshooting, for example, had for some begun to take on "a strange fascination for men of a sporting turn of mind," according to Confederate soldier James Wilson, and "no one seemed to feel any more compunction in taking a good shot at an unknown enemy than at a deer."[14]

Confederate soldier William Blackford was despondent after six weeks in the trenches, that "lazy, monotonous, sickening, murderous, unnatural, uncivilized mode of being."[15] Many soldiers also began to see themselves as powerless victims against the seemingly random and destructive power of the mortar (used to fire shells at high angles), sharpshooter fire, and land mines and underground explosives. Technology, for many, was rendering the agency of the individual soldier moot and challenging the utility and validity of the cultural standard of masculinity. In a war of attrition, heroic masculinity held less sway. Godliness, for example, did not even appear to offer divine protection. Writing about the Confederate soldier in 1864–65, Alexander Hunter recalled that "The soldiers naturally distrusted the efficacy of prayer when they found that the most devout Christians were as liable to be shot as the most hardened sinner, and that a deck of cards would stop a bullet as effectively as a prayer book."[16]

Generals in command at the end of the war appeared to grasp the futility of "courage's war" as much as anyone, perhaps realizing that the best mentality in a war of attrition was to abstain from any moral ruminations about its effects on other people. Grant, Philip H. Sheridan, and William T. Sherman typified, in their detachment from their men and battlefield violence, the "destroyer" general immune to courage's precepts. Sherman, unapologetic about his role in the war of attrition, recalled after Shiloh that the "very object of war is to produce results by death and slaughter." And during the Atlanta campaign he "began to regard the death and mangling of a couple of thousand men as a small affair, a kind of morning dash."[17]

As witnessed through the eyes of those such as Sherman, however, savage interpretations of war do not inevitably create antiwar sentiment. In fact, by replacing the heroic warrior's code of morality with a soldier or commanding officer who sees war and those in it as dehumanized abstractions, a savage perspective can displace morality altogether. Freed from the burden of morality and emotion, those such as Sherman could carry on war's business of killing more effectively and efficiently.

Yet while some within the military ranks can use the savage perspective to detach themselves from war's violence and morality, it remains unlikely that the general public would be more supportive of killing if it were presented as savage and amoral instead of heroic and moral. Savage interpretations of war experience, if represented in a way that exposes war's inhumanity, do produce a rather bleak and unromantic picture of war. In many ways, the savage interpretations of war more commonly expressed by Civil War soldiers toward the end of the war echo this critique: war seems purposeless instead of purposeful; representations of combat deaths emphasize acts of killing rather than dying; soldiers seek only to survive the horrors of war rather than fight to uphold an honorable cause; acts of individual will are rendered obsolete by depersonalized military technologies; and the total effect of war is dehumanizing, as those within it lose both their compassion and sanity.

Ultimately, however, savage interpretations of soldiers' Civil War experience are juxtaposed against heroic interpretations because this perspective contradicts the dominant public memory of the war. Soldiers' experiences of a savage war also illustrate the validity of savage, antiwar interpretations and therefore the possibility of their expression at Civil War battlefields "preserved" to their original wartime appearance. Although some might take issue with the tidiness of Linderman's division of the war into two distinct phases of experience—"courage's war" of 1861–62 and the "disillusionment" of 1864–65—there can be no denying that the war, for some, evolved into a devastating, dehumanizing total war of attrition.

Giving voice to the savage interpretations of the war does more, however, than create generalized warnings about the destructiveness of modern warfare. It also identifies, as one of its major causes, the heroic masculinity that uses war as its platform for self-actualization. By "separating" the war experience for soldiers into two distinct phases, Linderman underplays any causal connections between courage's war and the war of attrition. In what follows, then, I sustain an interplay between the "heroic" and "savage" interpretations of the war by counterbalancing the Park Service's own "heroic" interpretation of the battle of Gettysburg with a "savage" perspective. I place, at the center of interpretation, war's primary objective of injuring and killing. By placing war's savage killing at the center of analysis, I hope to show how this primary activity and objective of war typically is relegated to the periphery of interpretation and historical analysis.[18] My analysis of the Park Service's interpretation of Gettysburg is meant to illustrate both "representative" qualities of the Park Service's interpretation of Civil War combat in general and, specifically, the vital importance of battle of Gettysburg memory to the overall dominant public memory of the war. I begin with the most common and seemingly unmediated form of verbal interpretation of the past at battlefield parks: the verbal narrative of the battle represented through the genre of military strategy discourse contained in park wayside exhibits.

Verbal Interpretations of Combat: The Rhetoric of Military Strategy Discourse

The glorification of heroic masculinity is disguised within a genre of military strategy discourse used at Gettysburg National Military Park to dispassionately chronicle the strategies and tactics of both sides in the three-day battle. This genre proliferates in most accounts of Civil War combat, which creates a rhetoric of warfare far different from that composed through the daily journal writings and letters of the Civil War combat soldier. Regarding the genre of strategy writing, Elaine Scarry observes, "the intricacies and complications of the massive geographical interactions between two armies of opposing nations tend to be represented without frequent reference to the actual injuries occurring to the hundreds of thousands of soldiers involved: the movement and actions of the armies are emptied of human content and occur as a rarefied choreography of disembodied events."[19]

The genre of military strategy discourse is utilized throughout battlefield parks in the form of orientation films, sound-and-light shows, audiotapes that accompany the self-guided auto tour, pamphlets and brochures, park ranger talks, wayside exhibits, and tablets and markers. All National Park Service Civil War battlefields share a basic interpretive plan: as much original battlefield land as possible is preserved in order to re-create a narrative of that battle's chronological structure; physical structures such as homes and barns are preserved by the Park Service to help orient visitors to the battlefield and occasionally to tell human interest stories; Park Service wayside markers and (depending on when the battlefield was consigned) battery tablets and brigade markers created by the War Department are placed on the battlefield to create a chronological narrative of the battle's precise engagements and troop movements; and self-guided auto tour maps are distributed in the visitor center to help visitors navigate through the sequentially organized stops (generally between six and twelve) on the battlefield.

Rhetorically, military strategy discourse used in wayside markers relocates the centrality of battlefield injuring and killing to the periphery in six interrelated ways.

First, the markers condense the action of thousands of individual bodies into the form of one or two metaphoric colossal bodies, often represented by the armies' commanding generals, who always continue to "live" despite the death of many of the body's individual parts. Second, the markers encourage visitors to adopt the broad and panoramic point of view of the generals who represent the colossal body, which contributes to the abstraction of battlefield injuring and renders invisible the individual soldiers' often claustrophobic and chaotic point of view.

Third, by making injuring and killing seem like secondary objectives to the attainment of some other strategic goal, whether it be securing "high ground" or an ideological goal, such as "preserving the Union," the wayside markers successfully shift the focus of killing to the periphery. Fourth, the markers confront injuring and killing through the frame of heroic masculinity, thereby emphasizing honorable ways of incurring injuries and death rather than confronting brutal and impersonal forms of killing. Fifth, by depicting acts of killing or injuring as caused by inanimate materials (metal) disconnected from willful human agents, the markers shift the focus. And sixth, by utilizing, through quotations, words from soldiers and generals to support one or more of the aforementioned perspectives, killing is decentralized.[20]

The first stop on the self-guided auto tour is McPherson Ridge, site of the first round of injuring and killing at Gettysburg. A wayside exhibit titled "The Battle Opens" explains what happened there:

Forward men, forward for God's sake, and drive those fellows out of those woods.

> —Maj. Gen. John F. Reynolds, U.S.A.
> Commander, First Army Corps

On the morning of July 1, 1863, the bloodiest single battle of the Civil War began here on the outskirts of Gettysburg.

About 8 A.M., 7,000 Confederate infantry attacking from the west and north (in front of you) clashed with 3,200 dismounted Union cavalry positioned along this ridge. The cavalry slowed the Confederate tide until the Union infantry arrived on the battlefield.

By 10:30 A.M., the Union First Corps reached the field and drove the Confederates back in a bloody hour-long action here that left nearly 2,000 dead and wounded. Among the victims was Union Maj. Gen. John F. Reynolds, the first of many generals whose careers ended at Gettysburg.

This wayside exhibit does not omit the injuring and killing that occurred at McPherson Ridge but redirects it such that "injury is actively included and actively canceled out as it is introduced on a written page."[21] Reynolds, for example, is quoted issuing a directive to kill the enemy, but that act is made secondary to the objective of "driving" the Confederates out of the woods, their occupation of which appears as the central impetus for the "forward" command. Reynolds's directive also suggests that he wants his men not to permanently end the lives of other men but to keep them moving by "driving" them out, albeit in an opposite direction (backward, instead of the "forward"-moving Union troops). The objective of Reynolds's command, then, appears directed to reverse the Confederates' momentum and send them moving backward toward retreat, which makes the central act of killing seem like a means to a greater end. Forcing retreat for its own sake, however—without the high number of injured and killed preceding it—is not the goal of war, nor would it, in the absence of killing, ever lead one side to surrender.

As the exhibit continues, killing is both "actively included" and pushed to the periphery. The wayside first mentions that the battle of Gettysburg stands out because of its enormous bloodletting, but then it goes on to describe that process in ways that deflect attention from the manner, appearance, and centrality of that widespread killing. It accomplishes this in part—as all of the wayside exhibits do—by metaphorically condensing thousands of individual bodies into a few imaginary, individual "embodiments" that never seem to kill or die yet are capable of "slowing the tide," "pushing back," or being "pushed" and "driven back." There are few alternatives to convey, through military strategy writing, the large-scale movements of troops without using a general, brigade, or whole army as a synecdoche for thousands of individual soldiers. Nevertheless, not all of those thousands of individuals are killed in battle, and so the imaginary colossal body that represents the whole is always able to live, and although it might retreat or be "pushed back," it will continue to persevere, and even be strengthened by reinforcements.

Finally, the wayside summarizes the vastness of the injuring and killing but only *after* it is over, as the line the "bloody hour-long action here *that left* nearly 2,000 dead and wounded" suggests. "The characteristic act of men at war," Joanna Bourke states, "is killing, not dying."[22] Dying, however, has always occupied, morally speaking, a more sacred place in the heroic interpretation of war, while legally sanctioned killing largely remains morally reprehensible. Once the wayside shifts its attention to the "dead," then, individuals can more easily and heroically reenter the narrative, as Reynolds does here, a prominent "victim" of the killing.

The wayside exhibit also features the following short, two-paragraph description of Reynolds's death, which is commemorated through the frame of heroic masculinity:

Maj. Gen. John F. Reynolds, an 1841 graduate of West Point, commanded the Union First Corps here on July 1. While exhorting his men to drive the Confederates from the woods in front of you, he looked back (toward the Lutheran Seminary behind you) where more men were coming on. At that moment, a minie ball struck him in the back of the head. He fell from his horse dead.

The aide who carried him from the field said of him, "Wherever the fight raged the fiercest, there the General was sure to be found."

Reynolds's death is savage, in this description, but his death does not seem to occur in a war that is immoral and senseless. Reynolds's last moments befit heroic masculinity's ideal of dying an honorable death while performing individual acts of fearless valor that alter the course of battle. As if following the virtues of heroic masculinity in textbook fashion, Reynolds is struck down at the precise moment when he exhorts his men to charge courageously forward. The description is jarring because of the juxtaposition between the decisiveness of Reynolds's movements just before he is killed and the decisiveness of his death. The compressed time between life and death helps restore a final image of Reynolds as a fearless man of action, echoed by the aide who confirms his purposeful, indeed honorable, death.

There is slippage, however, between the heroic and savage interpretations of combat despite the exhibit's unwitting bias toward the heroic. One threat to the validity of the heroic ideology, if it were made explicit, is the perspective of the soldier who killed Reynolds—not because, in this instance, it would shift the visitor's focus from the act of "dying" to the act of "killing" but because the killing helps expose some of the ideological and strategic flaws of heroic masculinity. Reynolds was killed by a sharpshooter, whose role in both armies was often equated with cowardice. Discussing the infantry's attitude toward sharpshooters near the end of the war, Frank Wilkeson of the 11th New York Battery recalled:

> The picket-firing and sharpshooting at North Anna was exceedingly severe and murderous. We were greatly annoyed by it, and as a campaign cannot be decided by killing a few hundred enlisted men—killing them most unfairly and when they were of necessity exposed—it did seem as though the sharpshooting pests should have been suppressed. . . . They could sneak around trees or lurk behind stumps, or cower in wells or in cellars, and from the safety of their lairs murder a few men. Put the sharpshooters in battle-line and they were no better, no more effective, than the infantry of the line, and they were not half as decent. There was an unwritten code of honor among the infantry that forbade the shooting of men while attending to the imperative calls of nature, and these sharpshooting brutes were constantly violating that rule. I hated sharpshooters, both Confederate and Union, in those days, and I was always glad to see them killed.[23]

Wilkeson's frustrations stem from the decreasing ability of both armies to maintain, in his view, the clear boundary between moral killing upheld by "unwritten code(s) of honor" and "murderous," immoral killing perpetuated by cowardly, brutish sharpshooters. Killing itself, Wilkeson makes clear, is not inherently immoral, nor does the number of people killed matter as long as the unwritten code is followed. Presumably the massive deaths produced by the steady, unyielding, fully exposed assaults are honorable and should not be interfered with by the inconsequential killing produced by the sharpshooters, since "a campaign cannot be decided by killing a few hundred enlisted men." This is a slippery slope, however, for once one form of mass slaughter is deemed acceptable by both sides then resistance to other forms of killing will inevitably recede.

There is no mention in this exhibit of the sharpshooter who killed Reynolds. This helps heroic masculinity maintain its exclusivity over interpretation of combat and, in a larger sense, functions to uphold, for the public, a morally appropriate foundation for war. Although the ideology of heroic masculinity might inspire the public to support war and young men to fight it, this ideology conceals the fact that it imposes certain restrictions on killing. Indeed, many soldiers quickly come to realize that these restrictions inhibit the outcome of victory, as the side that first discards all of its moral reservations about killing will certainly possess an advantage.

The next wayside exhibit repeats many of the generic conventions discussed above and in such a way to reveal a pattern of when and why the values of heroic masculinity are used to inform the military strategy narrative. The wayside, titled "Trapped in the Cut," reads as follows:

Surrender, or I will fire.

—Lt. Col. Rufus R. Dawes, U.S.A.
6th Wisconsin Volunteers

The railroad cut visible in front of you was the scene of a dramatic engagement on the first day of the battle.

On the morning of July 1, a Confederate attack crushed the Union line here, sending the surviving Federals streaming back toward town (to your left). But shortly thereafter, Union units counterattacked, forcing a number of the Southerners to take cover in the railroad cut in front of you.

Despite deadly Confederate fire from the cut, Union infantry led by Col. Rufus R. Dawes and Col. Edward B. Fowler crossed the turnpike in front of you, climbed the fence there, and charged the cut. Although many were shot in the attempt, the charging Federals reached the edge of the cut and shouted, "Throw down your muskets!" Trapped between the steep slopes, about 800 Confederates surrendered.

Visitors are again invited to adopt a broad panoramic vision of the battlefield in order to understand the contours of each side's military strategy and by extension the commanding officer's point of view. And while that broad perspective does discourage visitors from imagining the war through the more chaotic and horrific perspective of the individual soldier, this brief narrative does give the reader a hint of the magnitude of killing that took place at the cut. In part this is because the combat evolves in a confined space, and the narrator has little opportunity to displace the violence by stressing each side's logistical strategies and movements. But as the killing becomes more salient, it creates a compensatory need for the violence to be explained and justified through the interpretation of heroic masculinity. Much of that is implied here, as the great losses on each side are offset by the narrative's central agent, Dawes, making it to the cut to force the Confederates' surrender after a bold and courageous charge. In a foreshadowing of trench warfare of sorts, the Confederates are described as "taking cover" behind the cut and damaging the Union men from that position. And although the Confederates' action is not defined as voluntary (they were "forced" to take cover) and therefore not intentionally cowardly, the values of heroic masculinity seem to favor Union motives in this skirmish, which is unusual considering the Park Service's desire to avoid favoritism.

The values of heroic masculinity are more explicit in an accompanying statement on Dawes that parallels the short biography of Reynolds from the previous wayside: "*Lt. Col. Rufus R. Dawes, U.S.A.,* collected an armful of swords from surrendering Confederate officers in the railroad cut. He had ordered the daring charge in which 180 of the 420 men in his regiment were shot down."

At first, the interpretation of the war as savage appears to be used to describe Dawes's confiscation of goods unessential to battle but of interest and value, a more common practice toward the end of the war. Linderman argues that early in the war most soldiers confiscated the outerwear from opponents who had either retreated or surrendered but refrained from taking possessions from the dead. By the end of the war, he argues, not only did soldiers take essential items from dead soldiers such as shoes, caps, and overcoats, but it became common practice to take items of value such as rings, money, and photographs.[24] Yet the confiscation of the swords of Confederate officers is more of a remnant from the "gentlemanly" war practiced by the advocates of courage's war. The explicit association of the charge with "bravery," used in this context to sanctify the great loss of life, supplements the heroic interpretation.

Conclusion

The wayside exhibits analyzed in this chapter reveal how the verbal rhetoric of military strategy discourse is used to deemphasize the centrality of war's killing and injuring. However, when these narratives do focus on killing in a way that might resemble or trigger the cruel or savage interpretation of the war, it sparks a compensatory need to portray such violence through the perspective of heroic masculinity. This interpretive frame, moreover, helps craft a public memory of the Civil War that sustains its moral purpose despite the war's (at the time) unimaginable horror.

Verbal interpretations of combat at Gettysburg National Military Park largely preserve a tradition of late nineteenth-century Civil War commemoration that helped restore the heroic masculinity of white soldiers and officers who fought on both sides in the American Civil War. In this chapter I have illustrated how contemporary park visitors are invited to use this national masculine ideology to help them interpret the battle's strategic, moral, and violent dimensions. In the absence of other interpretive frames, heroic masculinity assumes the dominant and "natural" perspective from which to analyze these themes.

I have introduced a savage interpretation of the battle of Gettysburg in this chapter not only to critique the practical and ethical limits of heroic masculinity but also to help prospective visitors "balance" their interpretation of the site with another perspective on the battle legitimized by soldiers' own experiences of the war. In the next chapter I will continue to emphasize the centrality of savagery in my reading of the Park Service's use of the physical landscape, monuments, and Civil War photography to interpret battle of Gettysburg combat on the self-guided auto tour, most notably the legendary Pickett's Charge.

4
The Symbolic Landscape
Visualizing Violence at Gettysburg National Military Park

How is battlefield injuring and killing represented visually at national Civil War battlefield parks such as Gettysburg National Military Park? This chapter addresses the visual representation of violence through the physical landscape, monuments, photographs, and vivid "word pictures" featured within the stops on the self-guided auto tour of the battlefield that follow those from the preceding chapter. By linking combat to a pastoral landscape, I argue that visual representations of battle at GNMP function to complement, idealize, and naturalize heroic masculinity. This pastoral rhetoric effaces savage interpretations of the war by contextualizing combat within a vast, bucolic, serene landscape, thereby fusing representations of the body (living and dead) of the Civil War soldier and the pastoral landscape into a harmonious synthesis. Moreover, by repeatedly directing the visitor's gaze to broad, panoramic battlefield vistas that replicate a commanding officer's strategic point of view, visual representations of combat in the wayside exhibits help assist visitors in linking combat to the pastoral.

The physical landscape, more so than other forms of visual interpretation (with the exception of photography, perhaps), appears to reflect a past unmediated by the subjective forces of history and human agency. Yet battlefields are designated, after all, as battlefield *parks,* and the beautifully maintained battlefield grounds, while undoubtedly a source of the Park Service's popularity, do contribute to its overall depiction of combat. The rhetoric of visual representation at a given wayside is also complicated by the combination of visual mediums used at a given stop, while each of those mediums is influenced by its own artistic and institutional conventions.

The next stop on the driving tour of the battlefield that focuses on combat, for example, seamlessly blends photography and landscape to complement the written wayside text. "General Rodes Attacks" includes a contemporary color photograph that provides a panoramic view of Oak Ridge facing south, with a cannon in the foreground of the photo. The cannon, which obviously is used to help frame this picture, nevertheless awkwardly puts visitors in the position of engineering the cannonade. Cannons are the only weapons that were used in the service of killing at Gettysburg that are "preserved" by the Park Service on the battlefield. Their presence, however, does not easily conform to a savage or heroic interpretation of battle. The savage perspective, linked to soldiers' experience of killing as amoral, random, destructive, and dehumanizing, would be more accurately represented by positioning visitors on the receiving end of a shell, whose indiscriminate damage defies heroic masculinity's courageous tenets.

Placing visitors behind the cannon helps efface the savage perspective, although there is nothing about the photograph that suggests the need to utilize the heroic perspective to make sense of it. The perspective is dehumanizing, to be sure, as it removes visitors by hundreds of yards from the injuring and killing while also inviting them to associate its cause with the lead shell rather than the human individual. This form of dehumanization is not savage, however, for it renders people as abstractions, thereby desensitizing, as opposed to repelling, visitors to killing.[1] In this sense, the positioning of battlefield cannons, both in photographs and on the landscape, is consistent with modern representations of antiseptic "high-tech" war that might help naturalize, for contemporary visitors, the ubiquitous presence of cannons at NPS battlefields.

It becomes obvious that visitors are invited to understand the combat at Oak Ridge from the perspective of Maj. Gen. Robert E. Rodes, not the Confederate soldiers operating the cannons, once the verbal interpretation of this site is combined with the visual. Once again, conventions of military history writing are utilized to reduce the armies to a colossal body, this time that of Rodes:

GENERAL RODES ATTACKS

At midday on July 1, after a lull in the fighting, Maj. Gen. Robert E. Rodes took position on this hill north of Gettysburg with 8,000 Confederates. Other Confederate divisions were converging

on the town from your right and left. The closest Union troops
were on Oak Ridge about ⅓-mile in front of you.

The thunder of Southern cannon positioned here signaled the
beginning of the attack. Following the cannonade, Brig. Gen.
Alfred Iverson's North Carolina Brigade advanced with other
Confederates against Oak Ridge. As Iverson neared the ridge,
Federals concealed behind a stone wall rose up and raked the
North Carolinians with murderous fire. More than half the 1,470
Confederates engaged were killed, wounded, or captured.

Rodes then regrouped and renewed the attack, bringing more
Confederate troops into battle. By 4:00 P.M., despite heavy losses,
the Confederates had pushed the Federals back to the streets of
Gettysburg.

One constraint of military history writing that emphasizes a commanding officer's point of view, John Keegan argues, is that it assumes
uniformity in soldier behavior and psychology and fails to account for
the fact that soldiers' loyalty often lies with smaller groups of men rather
than to the commanding officer.[2] This wayside, like all NPS waysides at
Gettysburg, reinforces the idea that all soldiers oblige their commanding
officer and act as one orderly, homogenous mass. It is difficult, however,
in interpretations of battle as brief as this, to create an interpretation that
accounts for the variety of soldierly perspectives while still moving the
narrative forward.

Yet it still would be conceivable to write short narrative summaries
of battles from a savage perspective without sacrificing historical accuracy or detail. For example, this brief narrative moves savagery to the
periphery by making the Confederates, who represent the subject of the
story, the passive objects of the killing. And although the Confederates
are involved in the killing here (they eventually "push back" the Federals), that imagery is softened by both the implicit justification of self-
defense (they regroup after being raked by murderous Union fire) and
the euphemistic reference to "pushing back" the Federals, which suggests that victory was achieved solely by moving living Union bodies
backward. Even if the subject and object of this brief narrative were reversed, the interpretation could portray the killing as savage by estab-

lishing visitors' point of view with the Federals waiting behind the stone wall to injure and kill the oncoming Confederates.

The wayside also relies on nature metaphors to describe human acts of injuring, which, when combined with other pastoral images of nature found in the battlefield "park," tranquilizes the destruction at Gettysburg while subtly usurping human agency by making nature an agent. The cannonade, for example, is explained not in terms of its effect on Union life but its sound, a reflection of nature's ominous "thunder." And while nature can be frightening, the most catastrophic force in this brief description is a man-made product, the "stone wall," which, in addition to helping Union soldiers "rake" the unsuspecting Confederates, foreshadows the earthworks and trenches of the war's final years. The values of heroic masculinity are notably absent in this characterization of combat as well, perhaps because the Federals' defensive position behind the wall defies the rules of an honorable frontal assault as defined by the heroic perspective.

Heroic masculinity is restored as the dominant interpretive frame in the next several stops on the auto tour that interpret the decisive third day of battle, this time aided by vivid "word pictures" that stress the battle's relationship to nature's beauty:

PICKET'S CHARGE

The flags flutter and snap—the sunlight flashes from the officers' swords—low words of command are heard—and thus in perfect order, this gallant array of gallant men marches straight down into the valley of Death!

—Pvt. Randolph Shotwell, C.S.A.
8th Virginia Infantry

About 3:00 P.M., following a furious two-hour cannonade, Confederate infantry launched a massive frontal assault from their ridge against the center of the Union line on Cemetery Ridge ahead. The Confederates who comprised this section of the line were Virginians commanded by Maj. Gen. George E. Pickett.

The Southern attackers, 12,000 strong, surged forward in a line of battle a mile long. As they marched across the Emmitsburg Road and approached the enemy line, the Federals raked them with deadly canister and musket fire. Nevertheless, with unsurpassed courage, the Southerners pressed on.

Pickett's men gained a small lodgment in the Union line at the Angle, but could not hold it. Casualties mounted, and the attack lost momentum. By 4:00 P.M. Confederate survivors came streaming back to the shelter of this ridge. The Confederate tide had reached its high mark.

Again it appears that heroic masculinity is utilized as an interpretive frame in direct proportion to the level of violence in a given battle. In this wayside, which narrates the most destructive action of the three-day battle, heroic masculinity is so transparent that it shatters the veneer of objectivity, despite the authors' attempts to allow the Confederate observer whose quotation begins the verbal narrative to contribute the passage's only rhetorical flourishes of description.

This interpretation of Pickett's Charge also is told from a Confederate point of view, and, consistent with Southern Lost Cause reasoning, it locates heroism in the fearless, steady Confederate frontal assault. At one level, the explanation for this bias is quite simple: the Park Service, in the spirit of fairness and objectivity, carefully offsets characterizations of the Rebels' crushing defeat with praise for their courageous effort. As discussed in the previous chapter and by other scholars of Civil War memory, this kind of "balance" helped solidify white sectional reunion while subordinating national concern for African American equality. Yet this wayside, along with the many other interpretations of Pickett's Charge found at the park, hardly seems "balanced" toward both sides. Its praise, after all, is reserved for Pickett's defeated troops.

That sympathy, however, would seem to have less to do with Park Service support of the Lost Cause political tenets of states' rights, liberty, and individualism than it does the need to exalt heroic masculinity and the morality of the war in general. Glorifying heroism and the morality of war is much easier to do when combat is interpreted through war's tragic deaths rather than its savage acts of killing. Park Service support of the Lost Cause, then, is incidental and serves not to exonerate the South for their part in the war but to memorialize a traditional form of heroic masculinity that can only sustain its legitimacy in the absence of savagery and its technological agents of modernization. The "word picture" created in the quotation that begins the verbal interpretation of the Pickett's Charge wayside is again illustrative: "The flags flutter and snap—the sunlight flashes from the officers' swords—low words of command are heard—and thus in perfect order, this gallant array of gallant men marches straight down into the valley of Death!" Certainly the Confederate soldiers are being praised here for their undaunted courage in the face of near certain death, but the author's excited tone seems to stem in large part from the majestic sight of this mile-long stretch of soldiers preparing their assault. The image is overwhelmingly pastoral and sublime, as nature is used to give aesthetic meaning and pageantry to the flags and swords of battle. Nature's significance here both eclipses and seems to control both man and technology, as the "flashing" sunlight and "fluttering" flags overpower the "low" words of command. The sheer spectacle of the soldiers' march, moreover, appears to blend naturally into the landscape, as Nature's guiding hand readies them for the march.

The pastoral mode, argues Timothy Sweet, was used by nineteenth-century artists and later Civil War photographers to associate the rural landscape with an idyllic, harmonious Union unmarred by the intrusions of history and technology:

> The pastoral mode . . . was still available in the nineteenth century as a mediating category that could resolve a perceived opposition between nature and technology. This resolution was often accompanied by means of a verbal and visual "rhetoric of the technological sublime" which transformed the conventionally nostalgic pastoral mode (with its anti- or ahistorical impulses) into a beneficent "progressivism" that soothed American anxiety about technology. The central trope of this rhetoric was naturalization, by means of which the factory and the railroad were represented as belonging organically to the landscape.[3]

The pastoral mode operates rhetorically in the quote that begins the Pickett's Charge wayside by casting technology and history out of the wondrous scene. The visitor's attention is drawn to the soldiers' glistening swords, to be sure, but this weapon helps contribute to the scene's nostalgia rather than detract from it. By excluding images of modern weaponry from the scene, the author both promotes nostalgia for an older form of chivalrous battle and protects the ideology of heroic masculinity from the critique of its usefulness offered by the war's more efficient and accurate long-range, lead-based technologies.

The pastoral mode is also expressed through the serene qualities of the preserved battlefield as a whole, especially at places like Gettysburg, where its gently sloping hills, mountainous backdrop, and small-town population re-create the pastoral "middle landscape" ideal. Sweet argues that this ideal, portrayed in nineteenth-century paintings and then photography, referred to rural, not wild, nature.[4] While the Park Service, as John Bodnar observes, helped respond to the desire by many in the late nineteenth century for a "scenic nationalism" by showcasing the natural wonders of the West, the vast majority of rural pastoral imagery was emerging from the South, not the industrialized North or the "wild" West. Romantic images of the rural South, in fact, were widely used in late nineteenth-century literature and painting to stimulate Northerners' sympathy and longing for the idyllic, agrarian South, which helped pave the way for white reconciliation. The Virginian Thomas Nelson Page, along with many others, helped sentimentalize reunion by portraying the prewar South as a land inhabited by faithful slaves and free of the dehumanizing forces of modernization. David Blight argues that in Page's hands, "The soot of factories, the fear of new machines, the unsettling dynamism of the New South could dissipate in the rarified air of gracious, orderly, old plantations; an unheroic age could now escape to an alternative universe of gallant cavaliers and their trusted servants."[5]

Blight was referring to the nostalgia for the wartime period that Americans could experience in the late 1880s. Since that time, the "New South" has continued to modernize, and wealth and power have increasingly been centered in urban areas, much like the North, leaving the pastoral "middle landscape" looking poor and destitute. National parks such as Gettysburg, however, seem to maintain the nostalgic look and feel of a memorialized rural South, thereby providing a space for contemporary audiences to escape the forces of modernization.[6]

But how do images of a pastoral landscape mesh with the battlefield's more violent past? For those such as George S. Patton, writing about his visit to the battlefield as a West Point student in 1909, the pastoral helps create nostalgia for the war without evoking its old, historical antagonisms: "The trenches are still easily seen and their grass grown flower strewn slopes agree ill with the bloody purpose for which they were designed and used. . . . There is to me strange fascination in looking at the scenes of the awful struggles which raged over this country. A fascination and a regret. I would like to have been there too."[7]

For Patton, and probably many others, pastoral imagery is appealing because it effaces war's savagery and uses nature to protect and promote a heroic interpretation of war as part of the natural order. The pastoral also shields Patton's imagination away from the presence and effects of technology (where are the weapons of war in Patton's imagination?) and the forces of history that caused two regions to declare war against one another (for *whom* does Patton want to fight and what causes lead him to so enthusiastically take up the fight?).

The rhetoric of the pastoral mode operates much the same way at Gettysburg National Military Park today, although I am certainly not proposing that the Park Service intentionally manipulates the landscape to produce this desired effect on its audience. The Park Service preserves the battlefield and cemetery landscape in order to provide a peaceful as well as historically accurate setting where visitors can honor the dead while also comprehending the course of the three-day battle. Nevertheless, one rhetorical function of the serene battlefield is that it creates a pastoral memory of the war that discourages reflection about the intrusion of modernization and its effects on shattering "courage's war" as a masculine ideology and military strategy.

One principal way that this is accomplished is by directing the visitor's gaze outward over long stretches of the battlefield in order to understand broader battle strategy and outcome. This can be accomplished through the use of wayside exhibit photographs, as discussed earlier, or by using monuments of the battle's commanding officers, usually positioned atop a tall granite column, to direct the visitor's eye toward a broad section of the battlefield. In addition, parking spaces at each stop on the auto tour are usually located at or behind the rear of an army's starting battle position, which provides visitors with an important strategic vantage point but removes them from the war's savagery. Figures 4.1 and 4.2 are two points of view that visitors approaching the Pickett's Charge stop on the auto tour, for example, are likely to see.

The cannon's presence in figure 4.1 would appear to position visitors

Figure 4.1. View approaching Pickett's Charge wayside and Virginia memorial. (Photograph by Jeff Schaefer, courtesy of www .myfamilyphotos.com.)

at a distance from the battlefield violence, thereby discouraging a savage perspective, but unlike the Rodes wayside, the interpretive materials at the Pickett's Charge stop utilize the heroic interpretation to help frame visitors' emotive response to the Confederate assault. The frequent references to soldier gallantry contained in the wayside support this frame, as does Virginia's memorial to Robert E. Lee (figure 4.2). The memorial is an obvious attempt to venerate Lee, the commander of the Army of Northern Virginia who emerged as the heroic icon of the Lost Cause. One of the important components of Lost Cause memory involved redistributing the blame for the failed charge from Lee to General Longstreet, who was widely accused of hesitating for precious minutes before reluctantly carrying out his commanding officers' orders to attack. The Park Service, however, does not follow this aspect of Lost Cause memory

Figure 4.2. Virginia memorial. (Photograph courtesy of www.nowpublic.com.)

in their interpretation of the charge, although they do allow Lee to express his deep regret for the defeat.

By placing the memorial within the battle narrative—as they do with most monuments throughout the park—the Park Service displaces most of the memorial's political commemorative functions and invites visitors to read the monument instead as a literal representation of the general's strategic position on the last day of the battle. The placement of the memorial within the battle narrative is made possible by the presence of two wayside exhibits that encircle the Virginia memorial and are dedicated to interpreting Pickett's Charge. Moreover, the memorial and the two waysides represent the fifth stop on the Park Service's sequentially organized auto tour, and most visitors follow this battle narrative instead of visiting the different stops at random.

The Virginia memorial, despite its more mimetic function, nevertheless still fits seamlessly into the overall heroic interpretation of the battle. This is primarily because Southern memorials at Gettysburg were allowed to possess commemorative functions as long as they memorialized actions that helped illustrate the battle's military history while refraining from commemorating Confederate political ideology. After taking over administrative control of the battlefield in 1895, the War Department decided to use the battlefield to tell an accurate and impartial story of the battle.

Using monuments to illustrate military history was not a top priority of those who funded their design and construction, however. Union regimental associations after the war, for example, seemed more interested in using monuments to glorify the sacrifices of Union soldiers as well as Union victory, while Southern memorial associations were interesting in promoting a Lost Cause memory of the war. Northerners gradually began to accommodate Southerners' requests to represent their own role in the battle of Gettysburg through permanent tributes to their own men, on the condition that proposed memorials were designed to illustrate military history rather than create shrines to honor Confederate political ideologies. Eventually the spirit of reconciliation led memorial commissions on both sides to support the construction of monuments to their respective heroes that were remarkably similar in their tributes to military valor and gallantry displayed on the fields of Gettysburg.

Virginia's memorial typifies such regional compromises made toward the end of the nineteenth and beginning of the twentieth centuries. In 1907 the Confederate Veterans of Virginia petitioned the Virginia State Assembly for money to help build a memorial to Lee at Gettysburg, and the assembly agreed in 1908 to establish a commission to administer the construction of a memorial to Lee and Virginia's soldiers. The memorial, formally dedicated in 1917, was the first Southern state monument at Gettysburg; it featured an equestrian statue of Lee at the top of the monument, supported below by seven representative Virginia soldiers. The memorial's final design reflected a few compromises made between the assembly committee and the Gettysburg Battlefield Commission. The Confederate battle flag, which was held by one of the soldiers at the monument's base, was replaced with a Virginia state flag, and the line "They Fought for the Faith of Their Fathers" was eliminated from the proposed inscription, leaving only "Virginia to Her Soldiers at Gettysburg."[8]

Compromises such as these help display how emergent national Civil

War commemorative practices were depending on the seemingly transcendent qualities of the ideology of heroic masculinity to heal once and for all the regional divisions caused by political ideological differences. The commission's recommended changes, after all, did not include proposed alterations to the figures of the Virginia soldiers and Lee, who was commonly recognized as the epitome of Civil War–era manliness and courage. The influence of reconciliationist sentiment on turn-of-the-century commemoration at Gettysburg is typified in this letter originally printed in a New York *Sun* article, reprinted later in the *Confederate Veteran,* which supported the need for a memorial to Lee at Gettysburg:

> The visitor to Gettysburg who stands on Seminary Hill sees in his mind's eye the figure of the general who directed the operations on the Confederate side. Why not a representation of him in bronze to kindle the imagination? No man who is capable of admiring the genius, courage, and manliness of Robert E. Lee, no less an American because he wore the gray, will be satisfied, when the ashes of hate are cold and prejudice had disappeared, to read the story of Gettysburg only in the statues of Federal commanders. What a reflection it would be on the tolerance, charity, generosity, and even the intelligence of the race? "What," the foreigner would naturally say, "you deny to the South, which fought shoulder to shoulder with you in the war with Spain, representation at Gettysburg in a series of monuments which are simply illustrative of that titanic conflict! Does it mean that you treat the South as a vassal and not as an equal?"

This letter illustrates how the typical sentiments of reconciliationist memory were being used to stake out the acceptable grounds of Civil War memorializing. Gushing admiration for Lee's "genius, courage, and manliness" is clearly acceptable, as long as those characteristics are embodied in battlefield monuments that illustrate the story of the battle rather than venerate the Confederate cause. Masculinity, furthermore, is racially coded, its whiteness made palpable by the author's reference to the message of intraracial intolerance that the absence of Southern memorials on Gettysburg's soil would send to outsiders. Southern monuments in the North, then, were deemed appropriate if they limited their tributes to the commemoration of heroic white masculinity exhibited in the service of battle, a tradition that remains "preserved" on Park Service battlefields today.

Without its Confederate iconography, the existing Virginia memorial's symbolism is restricted to abstract messages about white masculine hegemony, as the feminine state (the inscription reads "Virginia to Her Soldiers at Gettysburg") expresses its gratitude to her brave male protectors, especially Lee. Kirk Savage argues that the equestrian image of Lee and his horse Traveller illustrates his "power in repose," for it emphasizes how Lee controls the wild horse without exerting movement or force.[9] Equestrian statues of Lee symbolized, Savage argues, the calm and reassured paternalism with which Virginia would exercise its supremacy over blacks in Virginia after Reconstruction. On the battlefield, however, the Virginia memorial suggests how that subordination extends to the relationship between officer and troops. This relationship is certainly portrayed as natural and harmonious not only in the Virginia memorial but in Park Service interpretation of the battle told exclusively from a commanding officer's point of view. Moreover, by eliminating mention of the political, social, financial, or ideological reasons that led soldiers to enlist and fight, park interpretation implicitly suggests that soldiers fought solely because of a duty to obey their commanding officers.

Lee's statue is located on West Confederate Avenue near the spot in the woods where he watched Pickett's Charge, and thus Lee becomes a central figure in the battle narrative that is told through the two waysides at this stop on the auto tour. But by becoming a central figure in the Confederates' failed assault, Lee could easily be emasculated. Lee's heroic masculinity, and that of the Confederates in general, is clearly restored in the waysides at this stop, however. As discussed earlier, the verbal narrative in the Pickett's Charge wayside effusively praises the gallantry of the Confederate soldiers, while a second wayside expresses Lee's regret over the defeat, suggesting that one way to restore one's heroism is to take blame for the loss:

We gained nothing but glory, and lost our bravest men.
—Lieut. John T. James, C.S.A.
11th Virginia Infantry, Pickett's Division

As the Confederates streamed back across the fields from their failed assault, Gen. Robert E. Lee rode out to meet them. "It has been all my fault" he was heard to say. The attack had cost his army nearly 6,000 casualties.

With the failure of "Pickett's Charge," Lee sensed his opportunity was gone. His men were exhausted, and the number of dead, wounded, and missing was enormous. They could no longer take the offensive. The following day, July 4, Lee's men held their position on the ridge behind you, but the Federals did not attack. That evening Lee gave the order to retreat.

The retreat began in a heavy rain that soaked the downcast Southern troops. The high spirits that had carried them into Pennsylvania were dashed on the bloody, sodden fields of Gettysburg.

Defeated, yes, but this wayside certainly does not suggest that the Confederates and Lee lost their honor or manliness. The defeat, marked by unparalleled acts of bravery, was certainly an honorable one, as were the deaths that were incurred by the Confederates.

The interpretive materials at the Pickett's Charge wayside certainly seem to lend support to the claim that the Park Service dutifully follows a Lost Cause interpretation of the battle. However, their appropriation of Lost Cause memory is selective and only seems to be invoked when the ideology of heroic masculinity appears challenged by the war's overwhelming savagery and destruction. This ideology, however, constituted as it was by members of both sides at the beginning of the war and then commemorated in the period of national reconciliation, is a *national* ideology. The Park Service, for example, does not follow the Lost Cause historical revisionist tradition of blaming General Longstreet's indecisiveness for the failed Pickett's Charge, nor do their exhibits resentfully hint that the Confederates could have won the war if it were not for Longstreet's hesitation and the overall Gettysburg defeat. Park Service interpretation at the Pickett's Charge auto tour stop illustrates, in short, the agency's dedication to *both* historical integrity and the commemorative tradition of valorizing white American heroic masculinity.

Photographic Interpretations of Combat

The genre of traditional military strategy writing and the pastoral mode, as we have seen, represent important forms of verbal and visual interpretation at Gettysburg National Battlefield Park. These symbolic forms help preserve a heroic public memory of the battle, one visitors are invited to use as the primary means to interpret the battle and its place in the war and American history. The Park Service did not create this memory of the battle, of course, but they have helped naturalize and nationalize it, in part by excluding other interpretive frames from their own interpretive exhibits. Principally among those frames is the interpretation of the battle as savage. While this frame can absorb aspects of the heroic interpretation, it is used primarily to critique the limitations of the heroic frame as a masculine ideology, effective war strategy, and a vehicle for comprehending the realism and pervasiveness of battlefield violence and its relationship to evolving military technologies. One might reasonably argue, however, that the Park Service has but few or no options for representing war's savagery on the landscape, especially visually. Realism, for all practical purposes, cannot be extended to include evidence of the battle's destruction "preserved" on the battlefield. There are, however, a few existing options for visually interpreting war's savagery at Gettysburg, although exploring them requires looking at what is absent from park interpretation as well as what is available on the contemporary battlefield.

Photography is one visual medium that captured war's savagery, although it also utilized the conventions of the pastoral mode to represent the war in ways that supported the heroic frame.[10] Because Civil War photographs can easily be read as savage and/or heroic, especially photos taken by Alexander Gardner's team of photographers at Gettysburg, battle of Gettysburg photographs can add "balance" to the Park Service's overall interpretive programs.

The field of photography was just over twenty years in the making at the time the Civil War erupted. Photography at the time was commonly recognized as providing an unmediated window on the reality of its subjects. Gardner, for example, in the preface to his *Photographic Sketch Book of the Civil War,* argues that photographs have distinct advantages over the written word, as "[v]erbal representations of . . . places, or scenes, may or may not have the merit of accuracy; but photographic presentments of them will be accepted by posterity with an undoubting faith."[11] Despite this widespread belief, photography nonetheless had important yet subtle ideological functions during the war. Timothy Sweet argues that Civil War photographers, almost all of whom were employed by or supported the Union, borrowed the artistic conventions of the pastoral and picturesque from landscape painting to make war, death, and the landscape seem like part of a natural, restorative, and organic whole.

Yet a closer look at photographs taken at Gettysburg after the battle reveals roughly two different sets of visual representations, each of which invites separate heroic and savage responses. The photographs taken by Mathew Brady and his crew approximately ten days after the war tend to articulate the heroic interpretation of the battle, while some—although certainly not all—of the sixty or so prints of the Gettysburg battlefield taken by Alexander Gardner and his associates a few days after the battle ended help create a savage interpretation of the battle.

The celebrated photographer Mathew Brady assembled a crew of photographers that arrived on the Gettysburg battlefield on or around July 15, 1863. The thirty or so negatives that were taken by Brady and his crew were largely a collection of straight-on shots of battlefield landmarks from long distances that together helped craft a visual heroic Union narrative of the battle. Many of the battle of Gettysburg illustrations that first appeared in the August 22, 1863, issue of *Harper's Weekly* were based on Brady's photographs. Both the illustrations and Brady photographs prominently featured the Union folk and military heroes recognized in the North at the time. These included photographs of the seventy-two–year-old Gettysburg resident and "citizen-soldier" John Burns and two shots of where General Reynolds was purportedly shot and later died. Historians have studied these photographs extensively to verify their accuracy. William Frassanito, for example, in his thoroughly researched study of the Brady and Alexander photo archives, demonstrates how both men and their crews either accidentally mislabeled their pictures or intentionally manipulated their photographs' composition (especially Gardner), captions, and accompanying stories for commercial and patriotic effect.[12]

One such example is a photograph taken by Brady's team of a large wheat field where General Reynolds was purportedly shot and wounded. As Frassanito points out, Reynolds was killed instantly by a sharpshoot-

Figure 4.3. "Wheatfield in which General Reynolds was shot," ca. July 15, 1863. (Photograph by Mathew Brady, courtesy Library of Congress.)

er's bullet in McPherson's Woods northwest of the town of Gettysburg. Frassanito speculates that Brady, who was joined by a guide on his battle-field tour, knew that the wheat field was not the place where Reynolds had been shot since the subsequent photo in his Gettysburg collection is of a wood line near the true location. Perhaps, then, the wheat field photo was more widely circulated for commercial use as the proper lo-cation of the Reynolds's shooting because it followed more neatly the conventions of the visual aesthetic that could not easily be replicated in a dense and enclosed wooded setting. For our purposes, however, Brady's picture is significant for how it invites an interpretation of the battle as heroic and/or savage (see figure 4.3).

Absent from Brady's photo and the others taken by his team are the visible markers of the war's widespread destruction and killing. Also, of the three available genres of photography—portraits, landscape scenes, and genre photos illustrating the typical life of the soldier or officer—Brady relies most on the landscape scene. Borrowing from the artis-tic conventions of the landscape aesthetic in paintings, Brady's wide-

Figure 4.4. The eastern edge of McPherson's Woods, ca. July 15, 1863. (Photograph by Mathew Brady, courtesy Library of Congress.)

angle photo invites the viewer to use the pastoral imagery of the "middle landscape" as the primary context for visually comprehending Reynolds's death. The battlefield already seems funerary and sacred, as Brady himself gazes contemplatively across the battlefield. Like the rest of the Brady Gettysburg archive, this photo seamlessly fuses commemoration and history by attempting to visually record a chronological battle narrative while commemorating Union sacrifices by photographing the landscape to look picturesque, even sacred. This photo, which also included a second plate, was featured as a woodcut in *Harper's Weekly* a month after it was taken, making it one of the first photos of the battle to reach the wider public.

The photograph's peaceful and restorative quality enables it to conform to the contemporary GNMP serene battlefield aesthetic. It is not featured in Park Service interpretation of the battlefield, no doubt because of its historical inaccuracy. Brady's next photo in the Gettysburg archive, however, which does show Brady and an assistant pointing to the general area of McPherson's Woods where Reynolds was actually shot, is featured in the park (figure 4.4).

The photo is featured in the collage that visitors see when entering the visitor center at GNMP. It is accompanied by the following caption, taken from Lincoln's Gettysburg Address: "The brave men living and dead, who struggled here, have consecrated it far above our power to add or to detract." The line of Lincoln's Gettysburg Address helps underscore a pastoral and romantic image of the photograph and represents another example of how the land itself at Gettysburg is visually represented as peaceful and sacred. In the absence of the context of national reconciliation created by the Park Service, the photo and accompanying quote by Lincoln would function as an example of Union commemoration. The pastoral qualities of the Brady photo, then, naturalize the ideological qualities of the pastoral by introducing incoming park visitors to a photo whose subject, composition, and long-distance point of view reflect the same pastoral qualities as those of the contemporary living battlefield.

Eager to scoop Brady, Alexander Gardner and his team of photographers arrived on the southern portion of the battlefield on July 5. As Frassanito writes, Gardner and his men had a much different agenda:

> Of the approximately sixty negatives produced by the Gardner team at Gettysburg, almost 75 percent contain as their main subject matter bloated corpses, open graves, dead horses, and related details of wholesale carnage. It is by no means an overstatement to conclude that Gardner's prime concern was to record the horrors of war rather than the area's landmarks (prominent features, man-made or natural) or general views of the terrain. This fascination with the dead on the part of Gardner is of more than passing interest because it determined, in effect, that those areas bearing the ugliest scars would receive the greatest attention from the first cameramen to reach the field.[13]

Frassanito suggests that Gardner was motivated less by pacifism and more by notoriety; the first-ever photographs seen by Americans of soldiers killed in battle were taken by Gardner at Antietam in September

1862, and they generated a tremendous emotional response. Many were appalled by the horrific views of war the photos engendered, while others responded to them with a morbid fascination. Whatever the reaction, the Antietam photos brought Gardner recognition. Gardner, then, did not go to Gettysburg with the intention of using the camera as a way to chronicle and commemorate the battle as Brady did but to record its horrific aftermath, albeit in a way that catered to Northern sensibilities.

Gardner's group arrived first on the area of the battlefield commonly known as Devil's Den, which happened to be one of the last areas of the battlefield to be cleared of the dead, and they took most of their pictures in this area. After taking some photographs on Little Round Top, the group moved northward, taking several more photographs of dead horses near the Trostle farmyard and the building used as General Meade's Union headquarters during the battle.

Gardner's photos of dead soldiers and horses would appear to more readily lend themselves to a savage interpretation of the battle. Moreover, compared to Brady's photos, Gardner's appeared to be less concerned about telling a strategic battle narrative, commemorating heroism, or depicting picturesque landscapes. Figure 4.5, which Gardner did not include in his *Photographic Sketch Book of the Civil War* published in 1866, is one such disturbing image.

Without a context in which to place this photo, it largely invites a savage reading. Gardner, however, usually included a caption and, in his later scrapbook, a narrative description to accompany each photo. Reading the photo and caption together likely produces a different interpretation, at least for Gardner's wartime Northern audience. A romanticized vision of the battle is absent here. Body and nature do not seem to form an organic unity, and the close-up shot leaves little room for the viewer's eye to set the disemboweled soldier's body against a restorative, pastoral landscape. Yet it is likely that the Northern audiences that encountered this photo interpreted the body as "Other," a Confederate object worthy of enmity, not empathy or remorse. His body, it seems, is left to decompose in the soil, his death hardly a sacrifice. There are also no markers of heroism here, for even though the composition of the photo is deliberately manipulated to reveal a narrative of cause and effect (the artillery shell is placed next to the soldier's knee, while the musket directs atten-

Figure 4.5. "War, effect of a shell on a Confederate soldier at Battle of Gettysburg," ca. July 7, 1863. (Photograph by Alexander Gardner, courtesy Library of Congress.)

tion to the shell), there are no signs pointing to acts of honor, manliness, or courage that contributed to the soldier's death. The caption, therefore, invites its wartime viewers to see the war as *necessarily* savage, not heroic or even immoral. This is William Tecumseh Sherman's destructive war, not Robert E. Lee's gentlemanly version.

The photo, minus its caption and the wartime context in which it was first received, invites a savage interpretation of a different sort. In the absence of enmity and a larger strategic war narrative this photo might arouse feelings of indignation toward war as well as an awareness of the

Figure 4.6. Adjoining caption reads, "During the fight for Devil's Den and Little Round Top, scores of soldiers fell dead among the rocks. This Timothy O'Sullivan photo taken three days after the battle shows Confederate dead lying in the 'Slaughter Pen,' the valley behind you." (Photograph by Timothy O'Sullivan, courtesy Library of Congress.)

destructive impact of the artillery shell and the helplessness of courage to stop it. This particular photo, however, is not included in the Park Service's interpretation of the battle of Gettysburg. Very few of the sixty or so Gardner photos are incorporated into the Park Service's recommended self-guided auto tour of the battle. This photo is used in the "Devil's Den and Slaughter Pen" wayside. (see figure 4.6). Although it is not central to the wayside's interpretation, the photo and accompanying verbal narrative do provide visitors with a far different perspective on the battle compared to other park exhibits and seem like a "natural" way to interpret the confined space of the Den. The "Devil's Den and the Slaughter Pen" wayside, which is a short downhill walk from the Little

Round Top stop on the auto tour, includes a Gardner photo (taken by his associate Timothy O'Sullivan; see figure 4.6) and verbal wayside text.

DEVIL'S DEN AND THE SLAUGHTER PEN
"Awful, awful rocks!"

For weeks after the battle, a delirious Alabama soldier suffering from his wounds repeated these words. The labyrinth of boulders and crevices in front of you was known to local residents as "Devil's Den," a name that would become famous in the history of the Civil War. The rocky gorge to your left and behind you earned the name "Slaughter Pen" for the great number of Confederates killed there.

Late on the afternoon of July 2, Confederates of Hood's Division captured Devil's Den and the ridge above here in a bloody struggle that lasted an hour and a half. Devil's Den then became a pest of Confederate sharpshooters who took aim at Union officers and men on Little Round Top behind you to the right. The sniping continued until the end of the battle on July 3.

As historic photos demonstrate, the rocks of Devil's Den and the Slaughter Pen have changed little since the time of the battle. A trail beginning here winds up through the boulders ⅒ mile to the top of Devil's Den and a fine viewpoint of Little Round Top.

The cooperative marriage between death, heroic masculinity, and the pastoral landscape is violently disturbed in the "Devil's Den and the Slaughter Pen," at least temporarily. The most jarring images of violence are reserved for the topography, not human flesh, as lush landscapes and glittering sunshine are replaced in this wayside with rough, protruding rocks of all shapes and sizes. The "awful, awful rocks" bear the brunt of blame, it appears, for the savage killing and are the source of at least one soldier's post-traumatic stress. Heroism is absent here, replaced by the presence of sharpshooting "pests." Characterizations of the landscape, unlike the Pickett's Charge wayside, yield little in the way of romantic imagery, and the rocks and boulders seem to exert a powerful, terrifying grip over the men who are held in its abyss.

The furious injuring and killing that took place here would seem to once again arouse a compensatory need to invoke the interpretive frame of heroic masculinity to justify the morality of the killing while simultaneously displacing its violence from the center of awareness. That frame is notably absent here, which suggests that the generic conventions of military strategy discourse must somehow be inapplicable to this scene. In fact, the orderly movements of thousands of soldiers represented by the colossal body of a commanding general cannot be accounted for in the enclosed Devil's Den and Slaughter Pen. There is no room for the human eye to gaze out over long stretches of the battlefield to imagine the flanking maneuvers of the colossal body. War's primary objective of injuring and killing cannot easily be subordinated to a larger strategic narrative in the absence of its typical battlefield setting. Heroic masculinity cannot be utilized to valorize the bravery of sharpshooters hidden behind foreboding rocks.

Although the rocks and boulders in this narrative might appear more savage and infamous than the people hiding and dying in their crevices, the topography of Devil's Den and the Slaughter Pen nevertheless creates a greater opening for a savage and tragic interpretation of the battle of Gettysburg. The moment is temporary, to be sure, as the narrator invites visitors at the end of the wayside to resume the preferred point of view by following the trail that begins at the wayside and "winds up through the boulders ⅒ mile to the top of Devil's Den and a fine viewpoint of Little Round Top."

Despite their brief appearance, the imposing rock and boulder formations located in this shallow, tightly confined ravine help create an opening for a savage and tragic perspective that invites visitors to imagine war's killing and dying being executed and endured by individual human beings, not impersonal armies of bodies.

Conclusion

Even though there are a few openings for interpreting the war as savage or tragic on the self-guided auto tour of the Gettysburg battlefield, visitors conditioned to the ubiquitous heroic frame might simply interpret the fighting and sniper fire described at such waysides as "Devil's Den and Slaughter Pen" as cowardly or unmanly rather than savage or tragic.

The heroic interpretation of the battle of Gettysburg invites visitors to reflect nostalgically about heroic warriors who displayed unparalleled acts of courage against the backdrop of a picturesque landscape far removed from the intrusions of industrial modernity. In this sense, the Park Service helps provide the material conditions that enable so many to use Civil War memory as a haven from the forces of social, economic, and industrial change.

A savage interpretation of the battle of Gettysburg, however, assists visitors in critiquing the assumptions the heroic frame creates about the battle's temporal relationship to public memory, the effectiveness of the era's dominant masculine ideology as military strategy, the morality of war, and the centrality of violence. From the heroic perspective the battle of Gettysburg, and Pickett's Charge in particular, foreshadows an "end of history," not just of the war but of a style of chivalrous warfare that extends back hundreds of years. Read from a savage perspective, Gettysburg foreshadows a "beginning of history," not just of a downward spiral of attrition in the war's final two destructive years but of a future where many wars would be total wars of attrition whose precision, long-range technologies would threaten to make superfluous the warrior's code of masculinity. The heroic frame, in short, increases the distance between the war and the present, while the savage frame shrinks it.

Ironically, the site of the Union's most famous victory seems more hospitable to a Confederate Lost Cause interpretation of the war. As I have attempted to argue, however, Park Service interpretive exhibits do not valorize the Rebels' courage in order to validate their political cause but to restore white masculinity to its prewar (and post-Reconstruction) preeminence. If their representations of the battle of Gettysburg seem overly sympathetic toward the Confederates, it is because dominant public memory of a chivalrous, pastoral South is more accommodating to a romanticized, valorous memory of the Civil War.

The most powerful dramatization of this form of heroic masculinity, of course, is displayed in the Park Service's interpretation of the final, dramatic frontal assault known as Pickett's Charge, which represents the last vestiges of the gallant "courage's war." Read from a savage perspective, however, the easy slaughter of over six thousand Confederate soldiers in little over an hour signaled the beginning of the end of a combined frontal assault strategy and heroic ideology that did not often equal military success. Even though the frontal assault did not disappear from the war after Gettysburg, its failure as a strategy and as a primary cause in what was becoming a war of attrition was becoming increasingly evident. And although it did not fit the existing heroic frame, officers and troops were realizing that it was much easier to win a battle from entrenched, defensive positions than from a frontal assault fully exposed to the war's surprisingly effective weapons.

Through the eyes of some—indeed through the eyes of many Civil War soldiers—the application of a savage frame made the war seem purposeless instead of purposeful, dehumanizing instead of humane, immoral instead of moral, tragic instead of heroic. A savage interpretation of the battle of Gettysburg and the Civil War has its limitations as well, however. In the eyes of others, most notably generals such as William T. Sherman, war is necessarily savage and amoral; the sooner one realizes this fact the easier it will be to embrace war's brutal realities freed from the constraints of ideology. Despite its effectiveness as a critique of heroic masculinity, then, the savage perspective itself occupies a precarious liminal space between the dialectics of war as immoral or amoral, dehumanizing or desensitizing, inhumane or inhuman.

The battle of Gettysburg occupies a central place in the history of the American Civil War and American history generally. It also occupies a central and special place in the history of American public memory. Through its remembrance we attempt to transcend our most troubling contradictions. And while we remember the battle for its heroism, let us not forget its destruction; for through the "misty fields of valor" emerges both heroism and savagery.

5
"The Waters Ran Red"

Savage Interpretations of War at Cold Harbor Visitor Center

The number of battlefield deaths rose significantly in the bloody spring of 1864, as Lt. Gen. Ulysses S. Grant, Lincoln's choice as newly appointed general-in-chief of the Union armies, attempted an aggressive and co-ordinated strategy to destroy the dwindling Rebel forces and the Confederacy's will to fight. Responding to President Lincoln's frustration at the "procrastination on the part of [earlier] commanders," Grant forged a coordinated plan to prevent Confederates from shifting their smaller defenses to emerging problem areas. Grant would advance with Gen. George Meade, leader of the Army of the Potomac, in an attempt to pin Robert E. Lee's Army of Northern Virginia against the Confederate capital of Richmond; Maj. Gen. William Sherman would defeat Gen. Joseph E. Johnston's army and capture Atlanta; Cavalry Corps leader Philip Sheridan would cut off Lee's food supply and destroy civilian infrastructure in Virginia; and Maj. Gen. Nathaniel P. Banks was sent to capture Mobile, Alabama.[1]

Grant believed that the best way to defeat the smaller but tenacious Confederate army was to demoralize the South's capacity for warfare by destroying its armies and war resources. By ravaging homes and prop-erty, burning crops, consuming supplies, and disrupting rail lines, the Union army would, the reasoning went, cripple the South economically and psychologically, while subjecting the Confederacy to an unrelenting war of attrition that would bring an end to the unpredictably prolonged conflict.

The war's escalating toll on private citizens was matched on the battle-field by staggeringly high numbers of dead and wounded. The battles fought between Lee and Grant at the Wilderness, Spotsylvania Court House, and Cold Harbor in less than a month's time in May and June

1864 would result in the loss of over fifty thousand Union men and thirty-two thousand Confederates. As Harry Stout gloomily calculates, the figures represent "nearly half of the total Federal casualties for the entire three years prior. Shiloh, Antietam, Gettysburg, and Chickamauga had served as mere dress rehearsals for spring 1864."[2]

In this chapter I examine how, if at all, reconciliationist and emancipationist commemorative traditions are used to interpret the final stages of a hard and destructive war that many Americans would prefer to forget. I have selected Cold Harbor as the subject of this chapter because it typifies the hard, bitter total war fought in 1864–65. Additionally, defensive fortifications, trench warfare, and the prominence of the sharpshooter at Cold Harbor pose challenges to the heroic frame invoked by reconciliationist memory to interpret and commemorate battle. Ultimately, I argue, reconciliationist and emancipationist public memories fail to achieve interpretive dominance at Cold Harbor, giving way to more savage interpretations of the battle that mark the landscape as a fixed, static place of struggle and death. After briefly summarizing Cold Harbor and the events leading up to this brutal confrontation that are part of the Overland Campaign, I analyze the wayside markers that adorn the one-mile walking trail at Cold Harbor Visitor Center.

The Overland Campaign

While earlier Union commanders had been roundly criticized in Northern papers for their hesitation and timidity in deference to Robert E. Lee, General Grant seemed determined to remain on the offensive, bolstered by the knowledge that his army could sustain heavy losses as long as they remained proportionate to Lee's smaller, diminishing army. As Virginia officer Charles Minor Blackford sardonically put it: "In one respect has his [Grant's] campaign been a success: to kill and wound so many of his men required a loss on our part at least one-fourth of his, and he is a hundred times better able to stand it."[3]

At this point in the war, increasingly sophisticated defensive fortifications made offensive assaults riskier and more deadly. After his heavy losses at Gettysburg, Lee fought mostly a defensive war, and his seasoned veterans acted like trained military engineers, taking advantage of every undulation in often dense, tree-lined landscapes to create zigzagging

breastworks across a wide field of fire protected by trenches, hidden artillery emplacements, and abatis of spiked trees that concealed the Confederates from their Union attackers and complicated their reconnaissance efforts.[4] Lieut. Col. Theodore Lyman, General Meade's staff officer,
noted the speed and skill with which Confederates constructed their
earthworks: "It is a rule that, when the Rebels halt, the first day gives
them a good rifle-pit; the second, a regular infantry parapet with artillery in position; and the third a parapet with an abatis in front and entrenched batteries behind. Sometimes they put this three days' work into
the first twenty-four hours. Our men can, and do, do the same; but remember, our object is offense—to advance."[5]

By stretching the field of fire and concealing themselves in tree lines
and ravines, the Confederates invited Union troops into a deadly crossfire that at times turned battles such as Cold Harbor into what amounted
to helpless slaughter, thus earning Grant the infamous "butcher" nickname. The prospects of a successful frontal assault against entrenched fortifications at Cold Harbor were so dim that it led many soldiers to pin
pieces of paper recording their names and addresses to their uniforms so
that their loved ones could be notified of their impending death. "June
3," one soldier somberly wrote, "Cold Harbor. I was killed."[6]

Grant elected not to oversee war operations from Washington and instead made his headquarters in the field with Meade's Army of the Potomac and his 119,000 soldiers. Much to Meade's frustration, the Northern press, enamored with Grant and his victories at Shiloh, Vicksburg,
and Chattanooga, would refer to the Army of the Potomac as "Grant's
Army." Refusing Meade's offer to step down from the post of commander,
Grant would provide operational direction from the field while Meade
would maintain formal command of the army.

Grant's first encounter with Lee was at the Wilderness of Spotsylvania,
a thickly forested area of seventy square miles in central Virginia, located just a few miles west of the spot where Lee's army defeated Federal forces at the bloody Battle of Chancellorsville in May 1863. Grant
had no interest in fighting in this spot and was hoping, when the army
crossed the Rapidan River on May 2, to use a right flanking maneuver
to force Lee's retreat toward Richmond. Lee had other ideas, however,
and pushed the Second and Third Corps to engage Grant before he had
a chance to move south. The dense and rough terrain of the Wilderness,
Lee knew from experience, would blunt the North's artillery advantage

and splinter its much larger army by forcing it to fight in more crowded and confusing quarters.

The vicious fighting lasted two days, with the South getting some timely help from Lt. Gen. James Longstreet's First Corps, stationed twenty-five miles west at Gordonsville, to reverse the advantages gained by the Second Corps under Maj. Gen. Winfield Scott Hancock against the Confederate forces commanded by Lt. Gen. A. P. Hill. Darkness prevented the Confederates from pressing their advances any further, and so Grant, on the morning of May 8, despite losses that outnumbered the Confederates' almost two to one, continued his campaign toward Richmond, thus demonstrating his resolve to impose a war of attrition on the South's undermanned army.

Lee beat Grant to his destination at Spotsylvania Court House some ten miles south of the Wilderness, however, and ordered his men to build a trench line stretching four miles. The only flaw in the line was the mile-long advanced Confederate position known as the "Mule Shoe" salient that Union forces would repeatedly attempt to break over a two-week period. Under the command of Col. Emory Upton, twelve Union regiments had some initial success attacking a narrow front of the Mule Shoe on May 10, which Grant tried to further exploit two days later with Hancock's Second Corps. Hancock's men fully breached the Confederate line, taking almost four thousand prisoners in the process. Any momentum from Hancock's effort was short-lived, however, as costly delays and poorly coordinated supporting attacks enabled Lee to move thousands of soldiers to repair the breach and launch an effective counter-attack with Brig. Gen. John Gordon's division. The battle within the narrow horseshoe-shaped salient would rage for almost twenty-four hours in a wedge that was later known as the "Bloody Angle of Spotsylvania," where fighting was so close and savage that piles of corpses and wounded soldiers were trampled in the mud by warring soldiers.

By the early hours of the thirteenth, and after ten thousand men had been wounded or killed in the Mule Shoe, Lee constructed a makeshift line at the base of the Mule Shoe salient. Grant, determined to "fight it out on this line if it takes all summer," tried again on May 18 to attack Lee's new line, but to no avail. Finally, as he had done at the Wilderness two weeks before, Grant moved his army around Lee's right flank and headed another twelve miles southeast toward Richmond, where the two sides would take positions along the North Anna River.

Lee had determined from three brief engagements at Haw's Shop, To-topotomoy Creek, and Old Church that Grant was intent on securing Cold Harbor crossroads, which led to a network of several roads providing easy access to Richmond. Both armies received reinforcements; Grant's, however, were mostly raw troops pulled from their posts defending the capital of Washington and were poorly trained in infantry tactics.

Grant postponed his plan to attack Lee's right and left flanks on June 2 when he agreed to let Hancock's Second Corps rest after they had marched all night from Totopotomoy Creek. Lee took advantage of the extra time to oversee the construction of a curved, seven-mile-long line that Gordon Rhea described as the "most ingenious defensive configuration the war had yet witnessed."[7] Lee's army, Ernest Furgurson wrote, "Had created not one main line of resistance, but two and in places three, following the uneven terrain, snaking in and out of gullies and clumps of woods. . . . Given time, they laid head logs atop their earthworks, with firing holes and crevices in between, and cut thickets of saplings to make defensive abates. They placed their cannon not just behind their main line but also in works projecting forward, sited to fire across the front of attacking forces."[8] The Confederates were so well dug in, recalled Col. Theodore Lyman, that all a Union soldier could see when he looked out across the lines of Confederate defense was, well, "nothing!"[9]

Into this labyrinth went Union Brig. Gen. John Martindale's troops at 4:30 A.M. on the morning of June 3. Slowed by an unforeseen ravine, Martindale's division was cut down by murderous crossing fire from the Twentieth South Carolina. Columns of Union soldiers were "swept away like chaff"; the affair was so one-sided that Rebel soldiers laughed about their predicament and shot down almost seven thousand Union soldiers in less than two hours.

The attack was futile across all fronts, leading one Union soldier, aghast that his commanding officers' failed reconnaissance contributed to a poorly coordinated assault against impregnable defenses, to label it "murder, not war." Columns of Union troops were funneled into awaiting death traps. A Union officer reporting on Maj. Gen. William F. Smith's assault on the left side of the Confederate line described how "files of men went down like rows of blocks or bricks pushed over by striking against one another."[10]

Grant halted his assaults on June 3, but the misery continued. Savage trench warfare ensued for over a week, as snipers and artillery fire killed more men than the battles fought on June 3. Additionally, hundreds of wounded soldiers were left to die on the battlefield while Grant and Lee negotiated a truce. Lee insisted that Grant adhere to a West Point code of honor requiring the defeated to first raise a flag of truce in acknowledgment of the loss. Grant finally relented on June 7, a delay mandated by the strictures of courage's war that cost all but three of wounded soldiers their lives. Then, on the twelfth, the Army of the Potomac continued its southeast trek to Richmond. After an unsuccessful attempt to take Petersburg, a crucial rail junction some twenty miles south of Richmond, the two sides would settle in for nine months of trench warfare in which Grant would attempt to sever supplies to Lee's army and the Confederate capital of Richmond.

Commemorating total war as heroic and moral poses obvious difficulties, especially when it contradicts a cultural code of honorable masculinity. How does the Park Service, then, interpret a site that could ostensibly critique a cultural standard of masculinity and the war that undermined it?

Cold Harbor Visitor Center

Cold Harbor Visitor Center is one of ten units within the expansive Richmond National Battlefield Park (RNBP).[11] A complete tour of RNBP involves an eighty-mile drive, although the Park Service recommends visitors limited by time see four sites: the visitor center at the restored Tredegar Iron Works along the James River in Richmond and the Malvern Hill, Gaines' Mill, and Cold Harbor battlefields.

Cold Harbor Visitor Center (CHVC) was built in the 1960s with funds from the Mission 66 Campaign. The visitor center, which at one point held no enclosure, is suffocatingly small, and like many Park Service sites, CHVC lacks the federal funding needed to upgrade its facilities and interpretive exhibits. Visitors have two choices for exploring the battlefield itself: take a 1.2-mile driving tour that offers views of both Confederate and Union fortifications or obtain what a marker at the entrance of CHVC describes as a "more thorough understanding" of the battle by walking a mile-long trail starting at the visitor center. I elected to follow the more popular walking tour, and the insights from this chapter are gleaned from a close analysis of the more than dozen exhibits and markers that adorn that trail.

Rhetorically, the size, landscape, and interpretation of the battle at Cold Harbor deviate significantly from more popular sites such as Gettysburg. Perhaps most notably, the one-mile trail and auto tour do not encompass enough of the seven-mile-long battlefield lines to re-create a chronological interpretation of the first three days of battle. Additionally, the nine days of devastating trench warfare that followed the battle were static and therefore resist a linear retelling. As a consequence, the site fails to meet the Park Service's standard of preserving the requisite land needed to interpret a battle's full chronology, which in turn renders the accompanying military strategy interpretation of battle less central to Cold Harbor's message and overall rhetoric.

As argued in chapter 4, military strategy discourse represents a genre of writing that relocates the centrality of battlefield injuring and killing. Chiefly, it condenses the action of thousands of individual bodies into the form of one or two metaphoric colossal bodies, represented by the armies' commanding generals, who always continue to "live," whether in retreat or continuing to march, despite the death of many of the body's individual parts.[12] Using a commanding general as a synecdoche for an entire army also contributes to the abstraction of battlefield injuring, renders invisible the individual soldiers' often claustrophobic and graphic point of view, and makes injuring and killing seem like secondary objectives to the attainment of some other strategic goal.

While featured in the first several interpretive and wayside markers at Cold Harbor, military strategy discourse fails to achieve interpretive dominance on the walking trail and gives way to more savage interpretations of the battle and ensuing trench warfare that mark the landscape as a fixed, static place of struggle and death. As a result, the rhetorical form of CHVC does not follow the battle's chronological progression as it does at sites like Gettysburg but instead follows a structure of movement, stagnation, and death. Ironically, then, an inability to preserve the expansive battlefield creates an opening for more interpretive possibilities at Cold Harbor that would make it unique compared to other fully preserved battlefields, producing what is arguably a more harrowing and somber visitor experience.

The first marker at CHVC, located just outside the visitor center, introduces visitors to the battlefield through familiar military strategy discourse:

COLD HARBOR BATTLEFIELD

Here Grant and Lee, with combined armies numbering some 180,000 men, fought for two weeks in May and June of 1864. They came here directly after the battles of the Wilderness, Spotsylvania, and North Anna River. Grant stretched his line to seven miles here and attacked, but his assaults, especially on June 1 and 3, failed. Undaunted, he marched his army south to Petersburg and began the long process of cutting Richmond's supply lines.

Although these fields and woodlots around Cold Harbor witnessed the determined assaults and bitter close combat customary to 1864 battles, they also saw the evolution from open field fighting to trench warfare. Here the peculiar boom of mortars and the menacing crack of a sharpshooter's rifle came to dominate the front.

Grant and Lee are used in this first paragraph as a synecdoche for the fighting that raged between the two armies for two weeks at Cold Harbor. The two men are described as almost literally fighting each other in May and June 1864, while the Army of the Potomac is reduced to the figure of Grant and his strategy and actions ("stretched his line," "attacked," and "failed"), reaction to the fighting ("Undaunted"), response ("marched his army south to Petersburg"), and new strategy ("cutting Richmond's supply lines"). Clearly the task of accurately summarizing a complicated Civil War battle and ensuing trench warfare in a concise paragraph will, by necessity, reduce such complexity to a few manageable names, dates, and facts. At the same time, interpretation that makes repeated references to one or two metaphoric colossal bodies displaces the human consequences of the action's primary activity—injuring and killing, especially momentous at Cold Harbor—such that the visitor's attention is directed to the thoughts, motives, and actions of the war's famous generals.

The generals' absence from the second paragraph signals a departure from the rhetoric of military strategy. Instead, this passage seems to reflect on the historic significance of the fighting, marking it as the birthmark of trench warfare. Consistent with other waysides created during the Mission 66 campaign that anthropomorphize preserved land, human violence is displaced by nature as agent, as the "fields and woodlots" witnessed the violence and "saw the evolution from open field fighting to trench warfare," while the most destructive action mentioned in the passage is reserved for ominous sounds that metaphorically reference the "boom" of thunder and the "crack" of lightning. Cold Harbor's visitors, then, are initially invited to interpret Cold Harbor's violence and death—the battle's most notable activity and outcome—through the euphemistic lens of military strategy and the anthropomorphized natural surroundings and metaphorical language, yet without a justificatory heroic frame that would render its deaths as honorable sacrifices.

The next wayside marker sustains the juxtaposition between military strategy and the personification of nature, mixing descriptions of battlefield maneuvers with commemorative reverence for the landscape:

IN THE FOOTSTEPS OF HISTORY

This one-mile walking trail covers historic ground that witnessed two weeks of intense fighting in June 1864. It winds through earthen fortifications built more than a century ago. The Cold Harbor battle raged over thousands of acres, and this loop trail traverses only a small portion of the battlefield.

You can help protect the historic earthworks of this site by walking only on the trail. These fragile fortifications can be preserved only through a respectful appreciation of their importance.

Allow 45 minutes to complete the trail.

Interpretation here serves the interests of landscape preservation, as visitors are invited to observe and even commemorate, through "respectful appreciation," the "fragile fortifications" preserved by the Park Service as "historic ground." Nature again appears to absorb the physical and emotional weight of the battle as a "witness" to the intense fighting, and the marker's description encourages a more careful inspection of this important land given life and meaning by the fighting that "raged over thousands of acres."[13] Gazing outward across a forested area, the loop trail's series of seemingly endless, leaf-covered, zigzag earthen fortifications connect the landscape to the human hands that frantically manipulated its soil. In the absence of a heroic commemorative frame, this wayside's anthropomorphizing of nature—combined with a foreboding landscape—does not venerate the war's violence as evidenced in some exhibits and waysides at Gettysburg as much as it draws visitors closer to it. A drastic departure from Gettysburg's rural and pastoral "middle landscape" ideal depicted in nineteenth-century paintings and photography, Cold Harbor's forested trails are closer to "wild" nature, largely circumscribing the visitor's scope of the battlefield to the experience and conditions of a soldier's life for two harrowing weeks.

The next two wayside markers again utilize the conventions of military strategy discourse, which functions rhetorically to convey the sense of a progressive narrative while largely displacing Cold Harbor's violence. At the same time, heroic masculinity is again absent as a frame used to commemorate battle, creating another opening for nature to represent Cold Harbor's broader meaning and symbolism:

READ'S BATTALION CSA ARTILLERY

These cannon mark the approximate position of a four-gun battery belonging to the Richmond Fayette Artillery, part of Major J. P. W. Read's Battalion that held strategic points along the Confederate main line. The battery supported General Aldred Colquitt's Georgia brigade on June 1, 1864, and participated in the repulse of a Union attack that evening.

On the morning of June 3, Read's gunners were again called to action. Their intense and accurate fire was directed towards the advancing Federal infantry that were part of General U.S. Grant's all out assault against Lee's lines. Lieutenant Eli Nichols of the 8th New York Heavy Artillery recalled the devastation caused by these Confederate artillerists:

> "few men fell until we reached within [eighty yards] of the enemy's first line, when they opened upon us with canister [and] grape hurling it into our faces and mowing down our lines as wheat falls before the reaper."

WE MUST HOLD THIS LINE

After two days of bitter combat, Confederate infantry built their final line of defense across this spot. Remnants of that line are visible emerging from the woods to your left. Richmond stood only nine miles to the southwest and General Lee knew that he must hold here. A Federal victory could mean the destruction of his army and the fall of the Confederate capital.

Once completed, the opposing battle lines at Cold Harbor stretched nearly seven miles. You are standing at the center of the Confederate position.

Both waysides largely use military strategy discourse to mimetically re-create a macroperspective of events, thus marginalizing the experience that impacted almost every soldier at Cold Harbor. The first marker identifies its subject as the "four-gun battery belonging to the Richmond Fayette Artillery," which, as an agent in the battle that took place on June 1, "supported" Colquitt's brigade and "participated in the repulse of a Union attack," implying that the battle's violence was disconnected from willful human agents. The subject shifts toward the Confederates in the second paragraph, however, as the "gunners" in charge of the battery emerge as agents in charge of directing "intense and accurate fire" toward the "advancing Federal infantry." This wayside, interestingly, does not conclude by summarizing the results of Grant's attack and outlining his next moves but uses Nichols's recollection to bring the wayside's temporal movement to a halt. While Nichols's characterization of his own comrades as wheat falling "before the reaper" could be seen as a dehumanizing reference in its own right, the imagery functions not to efface technology's devastating effects but to graphically depict the suddenness and randomness of the soldiers' violent deaths, made more salient within an emerging interpretive context that has personified the surrounding landscape.

The second wayside restores a strategic focus of events along with Lee's expansive view, while personifying the Confederate capital of Richmond. Visitors' topographical and geographical perspective is widened to include consideration of battle lines and the possible "fall of the Confederate capital," which "stood only nine miles to the southwest," while strategy again informs the marker's interpretation of preserved land, as visitors are informed that Lee "must hold" the line near where they are standing. This "distancing" of the battle through military strategy discourse loses its interpretive thrust, however, as the next cluster of waysides invites visitors to collapse their vision of a landscape that offers little space, comfort, or solace for the living:

KEEP YOUR HEAD DOWN

This shallow, winding depression is all that remains of a "zigzag" constructed by Union troops in June 1864. In trench warfare, soldiers dug ditches, called zigzags or covered-ways, to provide protection from sharpshooters as they moved from one line of entrenchments to another.

Soldiers at Cold Harbor crawled through covered-ways carrying heavy loads of rations or ammunition, prompting one infantryman to remark that he felt "like some unholy cross between a pack mule and a snake."

KEEP DIGGING

These trenches represent a dramatic change in battlefield tactics. When the two armies met on this ground in 1862, soldiers fought shoulder to shoulder; victory was often dependent upon the success or failure of a dramatic charge.

By 1864 field fortifications played an increasingly significant role in determining the outcome of a battle. Despite the obvious advantage held by an entrenched army, Commanders continued to order frontal assaults against these nearly impregnable positions, resulting in enormous casualties.

These waysides, both devoid of an overarching military strategy narrative and heroic commemorative frame, suggest the inhumanity of trench warfare by describing how soldiers—none of whom is mentioned by name in either wayside—"crawled" through "covered-ways" to protect themselves from sharpshooters, making one soldier feel like an "unholy cross between a pack mule and a snake." The personification of soldiers as animals is reinforced through trench warfare's subterranean location within the dirt. The land here is not hospitable and hallowed ground but a refuge for vermin, leaving no room to describe the actions of commanding generals and the corps, divisions, and brigades that they lead, as the second wayside almost wistfully observes.

Most notably, there is no space for a heroic ideology to interpret events. Courage's war was predicated on demonstrations of manliness through unflinching, stoic behavior under the most frenzied conditions of battle. Modeling courage required the highest powers of self-control, and even though the soldier crawling on his hands and knees through the trenches might not have feared the sharpshooter, his maneuvering behind the cover of a zigzag would have certainly induced feelings of weakness and cowardice, leaving little room for the possibility of an honorable death. His attacker, the sharpshooter, could likewise do little to demonstrate courage and uphold a cultural standard of manliness; he was widely perceived as an ignoble coward who would "sneak around trees or lurk behind stumps, or cower in wells or in cellars, and murder a few soldiers from the safety of their lairs."[14]

The Good Death, writes Drew Gilpin Faust, was an important part of nineteenth-century America, and its theological foundations were appropriated in the service of civil war. The sharpshooter and his victims likely would find no solace in widely distributed pamphlets that outlined the contours of a Good Death. "What you are when you die," one pamphlet distributed to Confederate soldiers sermonized, "the same will you reappear in the great day of eternity. The features of character with which you leave the world will be seen in you when you rise from the dead."[15] Deprived of the conditions that made a Good Death possible, cowardly sharpshooters and their hapless victims were threatened to be "unmanned" by their experiences as agents and victims of death.

Proceeding through the walking trail, the next several waysides continue to depict events that seem irreconcilable with reconciliationist memory and its ideology of heroic masculinity:

A DEADLY DELAY

The Union assaults of June 3 failed on nearly all fronts. For the next three days, while Federal wounded lay untended between the lines, Generals U. S. Grant and R. E. Lee struggled over the details of a truce. On June 7, more than 100 hours after the attack, the generals agreed to a two-hour truce. Along one part of the line work parties found 244 Union dead and only three survivors.

One New Jersey soldier recalled that during the truce the former enemies were

> Talking to each other and exchanging newspapers . . . the works were lined with unarmed men, all gazing upon the solemn scene. The 2 hours soon passed, the signal was given, the men rushed back to their arms, and the rattle of musketry was again commenced along the line.

A LETHAL OCCUPATION

From this advanced Confederate line, constructed after the grand Union assault of June 3, Lee's sharpshooters searched for targets. They were near enough to the Federal line that enemy voices could be heard.

Between June 3 and June 12 constant skirmishing, artillery firing, and the deadly business of the Union and Confederate sharpshooters characterized the Cold Harbor fighting. Up and down the lines soldiers feared the work of these marksmen with their long-range rifles. One Virginia artilleryman considered the sharpshooter "little better than a human tiger lying in wait for blood."

These waysides continue the temporal suspension of a military strategy narrative and equate the loss of movement with death ("A Deadly Delay" and "A Lethal Occupation"). The inertia of the two colossal bodies, here symbolized by Grant and Lee's prolonged disagreement "over the details of a truce," functions as grounds for criticism, as the one-hundred-hour delay greatly diminishes the number of Union survivors and allows death to serve as the waysides' primary subject. While "A Lethal Occupation" describes the animalistic qualities of the sharpshooter and the victims of his prey, "A Deadly Delay" follows its pronouncement of Union dead with a soldier's recollection of a two-hour truce that suggests an indifference and numbness to both the scenes of death uncovered during the truce and the killing that ensued after its expiration. In the absence of a patriotic, religious, or heroic framework to confer meaning to "A Deadly Delay," both the soldier's description and its contextualization within the wayside read less like the kindling of genuine fraternal relations or a repentance of violence as they do a machine-like detachment from events.

The walking tour's final waysides continue the pattern of temporally suspending the movement of the colossal body to dwell on the omnipresence of death at Cold Harbor, symbolized by an inhospitable landscape that constricts movement for its trapped inhabitants and provides the Confederates with an overwhelming advantage:

THE WATERS RAN RED

This sluggish creek is known as Bloody Run in memory of the violent hand-to-hand fighting that occurred here.

Bloody Run flows east to west, winding through the woods. During the battle the brush-choked stream and its gentle slopes provided the only cover in sight. The open terrain in this area made the powerful Confederate defenses on the hill to your left even more formidable, and contributed to the overwhelming victory of the Southern army on June 3.

Similar to previous waysides that anthropomorphize nature, "The Waters Ran Red" fuses nature and humans through the imagery of the blood-soaked waters of "Bloody Run." Like the ground that it flows through, the "sluggish" creek provides little possibility for movement and escape, as its "brush-choked stream and its gentle slopes" offer the Federals little protection from the surrounding open terrain occupied by "the powerful Confederate defenses on the hill to your left." The possibility of heroic action in this wayside is undermined by topographical features that contributed to the Confederates' one-sided advantage. Deprived of the material conditions needed to procure a fair and square fight, heroic masculinity has no opportunity to demonstrate its worth.

While individual heroes are missing from "The Waters Ran Red," so too are its villains. Grant's reckless and poorly coordinated assaults of June 3, which helped earn him the "butcher" nickname, are not part of the description, and while the Federals appear to be the victims, the only possible source to blame for their demise appears to be the "open terrain" that enables the Confederates to gain their lopsided advantage. While it perhaps absolves human agents of the responsibility for Bloody Run, the Park Service admirably does not back away from interpreting the preserved creek "in memory of the violent hand-to-hand fighting that occurred here" and invites visitors to confront the magnitude of violence that turned the creek's trickling waters blood red.

BAYONETS ARE FOR DIGGING

This covered-way, constructed after June 3, connected the main Confederate line behind you to the low ground in front. A South Carolinian stationed near here recalled:

> To guard against the shells that were continually dropping in our midst or outside of our works, the soldiers began burrowing like rabbits in rear of our earthworks and building covered-ways from their breastwork to the ground below. In a few days men could go the length of a regiment without being exposed in the least, crawling along the tunnels all dug with bayonets, knives, and a few worn-out shovels.

NOWHERE TO GO

For nearly two weeks, from June 3 to June 12, the soldiers endured the agony of trench warfare. One Virginian recalled:

> Thousands of men cramped up in a narrow trench, unable to go out, or to get up, or to stretch or to stand, without danger to life and limb; unable to lie down or to sleep for lack of room and pressure of peril; night alarms, day attacks, hunger, thirst, supreme weariness, squalor, vermin, filth, disgusting odors everywhere, the weary night succeeded by the yet more weary day; the first glance over the way at day dawn bringing the sharpshooter's bullet singing past your ear or smashing through your skull, a man's life is often exacted as the price of a cup of water from the spring.

"Bayonets Are for Digging" and "Nowhere to Go" present a striking contrast to military strategy discourse while upholding a savage interpretation of trench warfare. The focus again is on soldiers' animal-like existence in the claustrophobic subterranean life of trench warfare. Commanding officers and their regiments are gone, their movements replaced by individual soldiers' recollections of the wretched life behind entrenchments and in covered-ways. Bayonets, which had functioned earlier in the war as a symbol of soldiers' gallant fearlessness in occasional hand-to-hand violence, are referenced here as a tool used in the service of defensive warfare. "Nowhere to Go" also rules out the possibility of the Good Death, for there can be little opportunity to demonstrate honor, manliness, courage, or godliness when a soldier's final moments come from a sharpshooter's bullet "exacted as the price of a cup of water from the spring."

Without the movements of the grand armies and their commanding generals to sustain narrative order and momentum, visitors are again invited to examine the remnants of isolated landscape features that serve as physical evidence to support the Virginian's graphic recollection of trench living conditions. Soldiers, of course, had to endure hardships from the war's beginning, but with the armies' movements stalled, interpretation can shift to the chief experiences of entrenched warfare. Finally, the Virginia soldier's recollections of monotony, wretched living conditions, and purposeless violence are allowed to stand on their own in this wayside without the reassuring frames of heroic masculinity or patriotic virtue. In fact, the wayside's bleak portrayal of trench warfare could conceivably invite visitors to read the auto tour's final wayside header and accompanying photo as tragically ironic.

THE ULTIMATE SACRIFICE

The losses sustained by both armies during the Wilderness to Cold Harbor campaign made the world shudder. Casualties by some estimates averaged 2,000 per day, and at Cold Harbor nearly 18,000 soldiers were killed, wounded, or captured.

While Confederate dead were removed and taken to Richmond, Union dead were hastily buried in shallow trenches near where they fell. In 1866 burial parties scoured the battlefields, collect-

Figure 5.1. African Americans collecting bones of soldiers killed in battle. (Photograph by John Reekie, courtesy Library of Congress.)

ing the remains and reburying them just east of here. Today 2,000 Union soldiers lie buried at the Cold Harbor National Cemetery.

"The Ultimate Sacrifice," which includes a reprint of one of Alexander Gardner's photos from his *Photographic Sketch Book of the Civil War,* presents an anomaly of sorts in NPS interpretation.[16] "The Ultimate Sacrifice" would appear to offer visitors a final memorial to the soldiers at Cold Harbor that reflects the perspective of a federal agency accustomed to contextualizing death within a soothing and stirring narrative of national progress. At Gettysburg, for example, with assistance from Lincoln's address, soldiers were commemorated through a reconciliationist lens that praised soldiers on both sides for their common sacrifices. Yet because reconciliationist memory glosses over the differences that led white men to do battle with one another, it must limit its commemorative praise to the gallant battlefield actions that fortified for posterity the dignity, honor, and valor of white men of the North and South. "The Ultimate Sacrifice," however, with its image of a black laborer posing with bleached skulls and dismembered body parts displayed across a stretcher, fails to conform to a commemorative convention that associates death's national restorative properties with gallant sacrifices situated within sublime and pastoral natural landscapes.[17]

Rather than seamlessly connecting humans, war, death, and nature into a reassuring synthesis, "The Ultimate Sacrifice" and many other waysides along Cold Harbor's auto tour suggest that war—or at least the type of warfare unleashed at Cold Harbor—is an *unnatural* event. Without the cues of heroic masculinity, whether they are successful frontal assaults, "fair and square" engagements, evidence of brilliant leadership, or decisive battlefield outcomes, interpretation yields to a frank and graphic depiction of war where men are reduced to animals, nature is cruel and inhospitable, killing is indiscriminate, and death often fails to uphold human dignity. This is not to suggest that earlier stages of the war *were* purely heroic or that acts of heroism and courage were absent in the trenches at Cold Harbor. Rather, the contrasting styles of warfare at the beginning and end of the Civil War produce rhetorical constraints that make some discourses and frames more likely to be utilized in interpretation, while others become more prohibitive.

As I have attempted to demonstrate, however, neither a heroic nor a savage interpretation of war is inevitable. The Park Service could quite conceivably extrapolate anecdotes to illustrate gallantry exhibited at Cold Harbor, for example, while Alexander Gardner's photographs of the carnage at Gettysburg could be used to illustrate savagery and destruction at Gettysburg National Military Park.[18] By illuminating what I consider the constraints that tend to bring about savage and heroic readings of warfare, my goal has been to open the way for more heuristic possibilities at national Civil War battlefields and parks. While mindful of the need to respect and honor the men and women who have served America's military, I have tended to stress a savage reading of the war because it has largely been marginalized in what has otherwise been a romantic and sanitized public memory of Civil War combat. By repeatedly emphasizing individual acts of fearless valor, gentlemanly conduct, and honorable deaths, popular representations of Civil War combat have tended to repress the centrality of the war's violence, the surprisingly accurate and devastating power of its military technologies, and the "total warfare" of 1864–65.

If battlefield sites are viewed solely as sacred places of consensus that preserve and honor the contributions of those who have gone before us, then some will inevitably view savage interpretations of Civil War battlefields as unpatriotic and degrading. Yet if viewed as sites of contested public memory that provide models for social and political action in the present moment, then a savage reading of the Civil War can remind us of the downward spiral trajectory that war, more often than not, takes: Stirrings of patriotic fervor and excitement often mark war's initial stages of preparation, as the vilification of an enemy produces feelings of in-group solidarity and a singularity of purpose elusive in times of peace; the prospect of violating sanctified moral codes through killing and dying requires a description of the dispute as threatening to one's existence and way of life, thus raising the specter of conflict to dangerously apocalyptic levels; and hopes for a short and dramatic victory are often dashed by the belated realization that killing sparks retributive violence, escalating the conflict and the means used to carry it out, all in the name of self-defense and often under the banner of God's benevolent support.

Cold Harbor Visitor Center not only gives visitors pause to consider the Civil War's final stages of attrition but can also habituate our awareness of the darker side of humanity that often emerges when leaders and their people select war as "a continuation of policy by other means."[19] Dwarfed in size and popularity by iconic battlefields like Gettysburg, Cold Harbor Visitor Center nevertheless stands as an effective complement to the war's romantic pathos, marking indelibly on its ragged landscape the tragedy that beset so many thousands of young men, struck down, almost 150 years ago, "in the morning of life."[20]

Conclusion

National Park Service Civil War historical parks and battlefields bring history to life for millions of Americans. By preserving and interpreting important national landscapes to reflect their appearance of years past, the Park Service stimulates our historical senses and enraptures the imagination. But if the history behind these landscapes speaks loudly and stirringly, it is because NPS historical interpretation is informed by influential commemorative traditions of the past that reflect deeply embedded ideologies about race, gender, nationalism, and war. These get transposed onto Park Service historical interpretation of the war and assist audiences in creating deeper points of identification with park historical and military narratives that can be otherwise dry and descriptive. Although their influence is profound, these commemorative traditions do not assert themselves forcefully on the landscape; they remain largely quiet and undisturbed, a seemingly natural part of the landscape preserved to its wartime appearance.

The Civil War has been the nation's most divisive, destructive, and transforming event. Those who control the war's meaning in historical memory have played a powerful role in defining the nation's postwar identity and outlining the scope and purpose of its democracy. Through its ownership, preservation, and interpretation of close to fifty historical parks and battlefields that tell the story of the Civil War, the Park Service remains poised to stare down the interpretive competition.

Yet the Park Service's voice is not inflammatory or propagandistic. In fact, in following the professional conventions and methodologies of the trained historian, the agency strives to read the past as dispassionately and objectively as possible. Traditionally this commitment to historical objectivity, combined with the agency's primary goal of historic and natural preservation, has created the basic assumption that a given park can provide its visitors with an unmediated window on the past. National Civil War historical parks and battlefields, however, do not exist outside of culture, and the attempt to "objectively" record the Civil War will inevitably be informed by both relevant ideologies of the present and commemorative traditions of the past.

Until recently, the ideal of objectively interpreting Civil War history had been kept afloat by preserving an interpretation of the war's meaning and legacy that was seemingly transcendent. That interpretation, forged during late nineteenth-century commemorations of national reconciliation, produced a convincingly balanced and "objective" recording of the war that distributed blame and praise equally to both sides involved in the conflict.

During this period, partisan memories of war gave way to a dominant interpretation of the battlefield as a space that could symbolize regional soothing and reunification, helping produce an ideology of white reconciliation through portrayals of soldiers from both sides equal in valor and devotion to cause.

Civil War memory scholars and an increasing number of NPS historians have observed that this segregated racial memory of the war helped sublimate racial equality as one of the war's unfinished legacies. Largely erased from historical consciousness, they contend, was an "emancipationist" memory of the Civil War. This emancipationist memory was commonly voiced by African Americans after the war to reinforce a memory of the war as a Union victory whose spoils included the economic, social, and political liberation of black Americans. That interpretation of the war's legacy and meaning, however, proved to be too divisive during a time when many preferred to turn their backs on the violent past and embrace a more tranquil and romantic memory of the war.

The emancipationist memory was more successfully employed in the late 1950s and early 1960s as a historical warrant for promoting African American civil rights. In particular, new interpretations of Abraham Lincoln's wartime Gettysburg Address were appropriated to intimate that black equality stood at the center of Lincoln's authoritative statement on democracy. By the 1990s, the interpretation of the Gettysburg Address as prophecy of racial integration and equality was so dominant that it, too, had become naturalized as historical truth.

An emancipationist memory of the Civil War, then, has gained widespread acceptance in recent years. Although the Park Service did not actively contribute to the diffusion and ascension of that commemorative tradition in the 1960s, they are now actively involved in telling the history of the Civil War from the perspective of emancipationist memory. In the late 1990s Congress decreed that the Park Service identify, in their Civil War historical exhibits, the legacy of slavery as a primary cause of the Civil War. The Park Service, whose national headquarters for historical interpretation is located in Harpers Ferry, West Virginia, responded to that initiative by using the local story of John Brown's 1859 slave rebellion as an opportunity to place slavery at the war's epicenter at Harpers Ferry National Historical Park.

I have argued in this book that interpretive exhibits at Harpers Ferry National Park and Gettysburg National Military Park tacitly utilize the commemorative traditions of emancipation and national reconciliation to craft historical narratives about the Civil War, while exhibits at Cold Harbor Visitor Center appropriate neither tradition in its blunt interpretation of battle. As I argued in chapter 2, recent interpretation at Harpers Ferry National Park uses an African American emancipationist memory of the Civil War to link John Brown's slave rebellion to a larger national narrative of twentieth-century racial progress. When analyzing the totality of interpretation at HFNHP, however, two broadly different interpretations of the town's meaning and legacy emerged. Exhibits created in the 1960s chronicled the history of preserved material structures dating back to the town's Civil War era. Although Park Service administrators classify preservation and interpretation as two separate functions of historical parks, the goals and values of preservation overwhelmed and dominated interpretation in these earlier exhibits. Subsequently, the "lived" history of important physical structures is featured prominently in older exhibits, thereby "dehumanizing" the town's memory and implicitly placing the Park Service in the role of heroic preservationist.

The park's recent exhibits utilized an emancipationist memory of the Civil War expressed by black leaders such as Frederick Douglass and W.E.B. DuBois to interpret Harpers Ferry's history as symbolically constitutive of emerging black equality in America. The emancipationist memory, furthermore, was used to reinforce a national mythic narrative of inexorable progress, identifying Brown, Douglass, and DuBois as its heroes.

The Park Service, then, appropriated emancipationist memory to interpret John Brown's slave rebellion as sparking not only the war but the larger movement for postwar African American equality. But while interpretation at historical parks such as Harpers Ferry can easily be altered to meet the demands of commemorative traditions now deemed status quo, battlefield parks seem less able to accommodate such changes. In fact, most Civil War battlefields reflect sensitive interpretations of battle that stress regional harmony and reconciliation between whites and are often the result of what NPS historian John Hennessy explains are implied conditions of battlefield conveyance negotiated with local and state constituent groups.[1] Since these are national parks, battlefield interpretation can only interpret the war as "American" by avoiding unbalanced criticism of either the Union or the Confederacy. Utilizing the emancipationist memory to interpret Civil War battlefields threatens to upset this delicate balancing act. Since emancipationist memory identifies with Union victory and rejects what it sees as the racist motives of the Confederacy, battlefield interpretation that is informed by emancipationist memory could ultimately criticize the South.

The tension between emancipationist and national reconciliationist public memories is especially vexing at Gettysburg. How, I asked in chapter 1, does the Park Service interpret Abraham Lincoln's Gettysburg Address? Do they use the address, as various black activist groups did in the 1960s, to emphasize Lincoln's desire that "all men are created equal," or do park exhibits select fragments from the message to commemorate the sacrifices of white soldiers from both sides who fought at Gettysburg?

The analysis in chapter 1 revealed that interpretive exhibits at GNMP created prior to the unveiling of its $103-million Gettysburg Museum and Visitor Center in 2008 selectively appropriated fragments of Abraham Lincoln's Gettysburg Address to interpret the speech as a commemorative tribute to the heroism and valor of white Union and Confederate soldiers. Dedicated primarily to interpreting the battle, those exhibits used Lincoln's address as a powerful expression of national reconciliationist memory to pay eloquent tribute to the sacrifices of white Union and Confederate soldiers.

The new Museum and Visitor Center, however, appropriates Lincoln's Gettysburg Address to identify slavery as the war's principal cause and racial inequality as its unfinished legacy, thus transforming GNMP into a site of contested memory.

An analysis of the commemorative traditions that inform the Park

Service's interpretation of the battle of Gettysburg is vital to this study because the battle is often where we turn to understand and interpret the war itself. The battle, commonly recognized as "the beginning of the end" of the war, invites us to use its story to teach us the war's larger strategic, moral, and political lessons. The analysis in chapters 3 and 4 revealed that the Park Service utilized the national reconciliationist memory to interpret the battle of Gettysburg, which functions rhetorically at GNMP to restore the ideology of heroic white masculinity to its prewar hegemony. And while this appropriation of white memory excludes the emancipationist commemorative tradition, I chose to resurrect a savage interpretation of the war articulated by soldiers from both sides to help reveal the Park Service's unique interpretive voice at this site. This rival interpretation can help visitors confront some of the more difficult historical and moral questions about the experience and magnitude of the war's violence and destruction that are effaced by the nostalgic lens of heroic masculinity.

Chapter 5 revealed that the reconciliationist and emancipationist commemorative traditions failed to serve as adequate rhetorical frames to interpret the hard and destructive "total war" of 1864–65 characterized at Cold Harbor Visitor Center. Instead, a largely savage frame is used by the Park Service to describe two weeks of failed assaults, unrelenting sharpshooter fire, and debilitating trench warfare that fail to model the ideology of heroic masculinity as constituted by reconciliationist memory. Freed from the constraints that have enabled the war's dominant public memories to justify the war's violence as serving the restorative purpose of unity and a renewed commitment to racial equality, Cold Harbor leverages an effective critique of exhibits and battlefields that sanctify the war's violence. Cold Harbor Visitor Center's savage interpretation is made possible, I argue, not only by Cold Harbor's bitter and inconclusive fighting but by the absence of a fully preserved battlefield that limits the utility of military strategy discourse to narrate the course of battle. As a result, the rhetorical form of CHVC does not follow the battle's chronological progression as it does at sites like Gettysburg but instead follows a structure of movement, stagnation, and death.

The existence of two rival interpretations of the meaning and legacy of the Civil War—as well as their occasional absence—raises several important questions for this and other studies of Civil War memory. How does the Park Service utilize the emancipationist and national reconciliationist commemorative traditions in their interpretive history programs? Does one commemorative tradition assume a position of interpretive dominance over the other? If so, is that commemorative tradition "natural" or invisible at NPS Civil War historical parks and battlefields while the other appears as a strategic rhetorical construct? Does the existence of two countermemories open a space for a critique of each by the other? How are visitors invited to use these commemorative traditions to shape their perceptions of the war's important themes and legacies? What conditions limit the utility of reconciliationist and emancipationist memories as frames used to interpret the war, and what alternate meanings are generated from interpretations freed from these two powerful commemorative traditions?

As the Park Service looks at the future of their Civil War interpretive programs, they see the need to incorporate emancipationist memory into historical narratives of the war. Yet the diffusion of reconciliationist memory is so profound and widespread at national Civil War sites— especially battlefields—that it remains to be seen if emancipationist memory will be forced to comport with the larger cultural narrative of reconciliation. In this expanded version of national reconciliation, African American soldiers could be praised for the bravery and valor they exhibited for their cause, and the war's romantic nostalgia would be extended to African American visitors as well. A revised reconciliationist memory of the war could also obscure or gloss over the historical contradiction between emancipationist and reconciliationist memory. It is conceivable that, having co-opted its interpretive competition, the revised reconciliationist interpretation would be written back into Civil War memory in order to erase the real history of white hegemony and replace it with a harmonious narrative of heroic interracial masculinity.

I certainly am not suggesting that the Park Service will intentionally structure their future historical narratives around their own ideological proclivities. Rather, an expanded narrative of national reconciliation could emerge at national Civil War battlefields and parks because it will best meet the perceived criteria for historical accuracy and patriotic veneration. Practical matters of "fairness" will also remain. A truly emancipationist memory of battle, for example, could distinctly favor the Union cause, thereby rupturing the Park Service's delicate "balance" of distributing praise equally to the North and the South.

Inclusion of the emancipationist memory, however, will be empowering no matter how these two commemorative traditions are intertwined. Featured prominently on the Park Service's webpage are the words of Frederick Douglass: "Once let the black man get upon his person the brass letters, U.S., let him get an eagle on his button, and a musket on his shoulder and bullets in his pockets, and there is no power on earth which can deny that he has earned the right to citizenship in the United States." The power of the image of the former disenfranchised slave fighting to secure his own freedom is unquestioned. As Kirk Savage has observed, African Americans who fought in the war should be memorialized because they fought to uphold a cause befitting the democratic ideal of freedom.

Yet as discussed in chapter 5, even with the emancipationist and reconciliationist commemorative traditions in place at Civil War battlefields and parks, some of the war's more confounding and unsettling legacies could continue to be forgotten rather than remembered and debated. One such view is an interpretation of the Civil War as a hard, savage war of attrition that witnessed the emergence of devastating new technologies that killed men in unprecedented numbers, while foreshadowing the total wars of the twentieth century that would make the wanton destruction of land, livestock, and ordinary citizens a prerequisite to military victory. While both the reconciliationist and emancipationist commemorative traditions justify the war's violence by harnessing its regenerative and redemptive messages of intraracial unity and racial equality, battlefields such as Cold Harbor, removed from the interpretive constraints of these traditions, can serve as a valuable antidote to the seductive allure of a romanticized war.

The loss of 620,000 human lives will forever lead Americans to rightfully define those deaths as meaningful sacrifices, whether the cause is preserving the Union, reclaiming heroic masculinity, or renewing the commitment to racial equality. Yet one also wonders if some of our fallen heroes, in the moment of their last breath, would have found it so dishonorable to sustain a tragic memory of that conflict that could help limit war's recurrence, saving our sons and daughters from a similar fate.

As they face the future, the Park Service will undoubtedly continue to do their best to interpret the past with the appropriate mix of veneration and education. "If we are good at what we do," the Park Service's John Hennessey has argued, "we can do our part to save the nation and facilitate good conversation."[2] It is my hope that by illuminating the Park Service's own interpretive voice at national Civil War battlefields and parks, this book has made a meaningful contribution to that conversation, assisting scholars, Park Service personnel, park visitors, and students alike in their ongoing discussions and debates about the meanings and legacies of the nation's most cataclysmic and transformative event.

Notes

Introduction

1. These objectives are outlined by former National Park Service assistant director Robert M. Utley in Edward Linenthal's *Sacred Ground: Americans and Their Battlefields* (Urbana: University of Illinois Press, 1991), ix–x.

2. As of December 2007. A complete list of Park Service sites can be found on the National Park Service home page at http://www.nps.gov (accessed April 30, 2012).

3. Rhetorical scholars in particular have begun in recent years to debunk the seemingly transparent and universal messages contained in Park Service preservation of historic and natural spaces of national significance, while scholars in the fields of social, public, and environmental history have tended to judge the Park Service according to the agency's own preservation standards. Environmental scholars have analyzed deeper meanings constituted through the Park Service's preservation of its "natural" parks like Yosemite and the Great Smoky Mountains National Park. See, for example, Kevin Michael DeLuca and Anne Teresa Demo, "Imaging Nature: Yosemite, and the Birth of Environmentalism," *Critical Studies in Media Communication* 17 (2000): 241–60; and Bruce Weaver, "What to Do with the Mountain People? The Darker Side of the Successful Campaign to Establish the Great Smoky Mountains National Park," in *The Symbolic Earth: Discourse and Our Creation of the Environment,* ed. James G. Cantrill and Christine L. Oravec (Lexington: University of Kentucky Press, 1996). Rhetorical scholars have also turned their attention to the critical analysis of historical memory sites, some of which are preserved and interpreted by the Park Service. See, for example, Bernard J. Armada, "Memorial Agon: An Interpretive Tour of the National Civil Rights Museum," *Southern Communication Journal* 63 (1998): 235–43; Carole Blair, Marsha S. Jeppeson, and Enrico Pucci Jr., "Public Memorializing in Postmodernity: The Vietnam Veterans Memorial as Prototype," *Quarterly Journal of Speech* 77 (1991): 263–88; Carole Blair and Neil Michel, "Commemorating in the Theme Park Zone: Reading the Astronauts Memorial," in *At the Intersection: Cultural Studies and Rhetorical Studies,* ed. Thomas Rosteck (New York: Guilford, 1999), 29–83; Carole Blair and Neil Michel, "Reproducing Civil Rights Tactics: The Rhetorical Performances of the Civil Rights

Memorial," *Rhetoric Society Quarterly* 30 (1999): 31–55; A. Cheree Carlson and John E. Hocking, "Strategies of Redemption at the Vietnam Veterans' Memorial," *Western Journal of Speech Communication* 52 (1988): 203–15; Victoria J. Gallagher, "Memory and Reconciliation in the Birmingham Civil Rights Institute," *Rhetoric and Public Affairs* 2 (1999): 303–20; Victoria J. Gallagher, "Remembering Together: Rhetorical Integration and the Case of the Martin Luther King, Jr. Memorial," *Southern Communication Journal* 60 (1995): 109–19; Cheryl R. Jorgensen-Earp and Lori A. Lanzilotti, "Public Memory and Private Grief: The Construction of Shrines at the Sites of Public Tragedy," *Quarterly Journal of Speech* 84 (1998): 150–70; and Elizabethada A. Wright, "Rhetorical Spaces in Memorial Places: The Cemetery as a Rhetorical Memory Place/Space," *Rhetoric Society Quarterly* 35 (2005): 51–81.

4. Quoted in Linenthal, *Sacred Ground*, x.

5. Much of this scholarship describes Park Service forays into natural preservation, which preceded historical preservation and interpretation by about twenty-five years. See William C. Everhart, *The National Park Service* (Boulder, CO: Westview Press, 1983); and Alfred Runte, *National Parks: The American Experience* (Lincoln: University of Nebraska Press, 1987). Scholarship on Park Service historical sites outside the field of rhetorical studies also appears to emphasize preservation over interpretation by chronicling how the argumentative tension between preservation and economic growth has been managed in different disputes involving the Park Service. See, for example, Georgie Boge and Margie Holder Boge, *Paving Over the Past: A History and Guide to Civil War Battlefield Preservation* (Washington, DC: Island Press, 1993); and Frances H. Kennedy, *Dollar$ and Sense of Battlefield Preservation: The Economic Benefits of Protecting Civil War Battlefields* (Washington, DC: Preservation Press, 1994).

6. Popular critiques of the Park Service have tended to adopt the Park Service's own criteria of emphasizing the accuracy of preservation efforts. See, for example, James W. Loewen, *Lies across America: What Our Historic Sites Get Wrong* (New York: New Press, 1999).

7. I have in mind here much of Carole Blair's work on commemorative monuments and memorials. Blair, Jeppeson, and Pucci, "Public Memorializing in Postmodernity"; Blair and Michel, "Commemorating in the Theme Park Zone"; Blair and Michel, "Reproducing Civil Rights Tactics." My understanding of a rhetorical approach to public memory is informed by Stephen Browne's observation that "to understand public memory, is to first understand the symbolic processes through which it is constructed." Browne, "Reading, Rhetoric, and the Texture of Public Memory," *Quarterly Journal of Speech* 81 (1995): 257–65.

8. See, for example, Dwight Pitcaithley, "'A Cosmic Threat': The National Park Service Addresses the Causes of the American Civil War," in *Slavery and Public History*, ed. James O. Horton and Lois E. Horton (New York: New Press, 2006). For a comprehensive overview of the Park Service's collaboration with leading scholars to review the agency's interpretation of Civil War parks and battlefields, see Robert

K. Sutton, ed., *Rally on the High Ground: The National Park Service Symposium on the Civil War, Ford's Theatre, May 8 and 9, 2000* (Eastern National, 2001).

9. Scott Hartwig, private conversation with the author, February 8, 2007.

10. John Hennessy, private conversation with the author, August 10, 2009.

11. Alice Fahs, "The Feminized Civil War: Gender, Northern Popular Literature, and the Memory of the War, 1861–1900," *Journal of American History* 85 (1999): 1493.

12. Although there have not been any studies that directly address the Park Service's role in Civil War memorializing, other scholars have addressed how the war has been interpreted in public space. Among the most comprehensive of these studies is Kirk Savage's *Standing Soldiers, Kneeling Slaves: Race, War, and Monument in Nineteenth-Century America* (Princeton: Princeton University Press, 1997). Edward Linenthal analyzes how people have used Park Service battlefields as a way to contest their meaning, but he does not specifically analyze Park Service representations of the battles themselves. See Linenthal, *Sacred Ground*.

13. David Blight argues that Frederick Douglass was one individual who was acutely aware of how control over postwar policy would be won by those who could gain interpretive dominance over the war's memory. Blight, "'For Something beyond the Battlefield': Frederick Douglass and the Struggle for the Memory of the Civil War," *Journal of American History* 75 (1989): 1156–78.

14. Maurice Halbwachs is widely recognized as the first scholar to describe, in detail, how "presentist" concerns inevitably shape memories about the past. Halbwachs, *On Collective Memory,* trans. Lewis A. Coser (Chicago: University of Chicago Press, 1992), trans. of *Les cadres sociaux de la mémoire* (Paris: Presses Universitaires de France, 1952).

15. Kendall R. Phillips captures this reciprocal relationship between public memories and culture: "These [public] memories that both constitute our sense of collectivity and are constituted by our togetherness are thus deeply implicated in our persuasive activities and in the underlying assumptions and experiences upon which we build meanings and reasons." See Phillips, *Framing Public Memory* (Tuscaloosa: University of Alabama Press, 2004), 3.

16. Linenthal, *Sacred Ground,* 93.

17. Memory scholars have, especially in the years since 2000, examined Civil War memorializing more closely at iconic places like Gettysburg, although Park Service representations of the past have not been the central focus of these studies. Moreover, scholarship on Civil War commemoration can reflect different methodological and disciplinary approaches. Some historians, for example, equate memory with "myth" and advocate substituting false history with a more "objective" historical record. See, for example, Thomas A. Desjardin, *These Honored Dead: How the Story of Gettysburg Shaped American Memory* (Cambridge, MA: Da Capo Press, 2003). Conversely, other historians attend closely to the textual dynamics of socially constructed Civil War memories and histories. For a provocative examination of the relationship between consumerism and Gettysburg public memory, see Jim Weeks, *Gettysburg: Memory,*

Market, and an American Shrine (Princeton: Princeton University Press, 2003). For a recent look at the role of American cinema and popular art in perpetuating a total of four interpretations of the Civil War, see Gary W. Gallagher, *Causes Won, Lost, and Forgotten: How Hollywood and Popular Art Shape What We Know about the Civil War* (Chapel Hill: University of North Carolina Press, 2008). There have been numerous articles and books written on Civil War memorializing prior to World War I. See Thomas W. Benson, "FDR at Gettysburg: The New Deal and the Rhetoric of Presidential Leadership," in *The Rhetoric of Presidential Leadership,* ed. Leroy Dorsey (College Station: Texas A&M University Press, 2002), 145–83; Blight, " 'For Something beyond the Battlefield' "; Fahs, "The Feminized Civil War"; Gaines M. Foster, *Ghosts of the Confederacy: Defeat, the Lost Cause, and the Emergence of the New South* (New York: Oxford University Press, 1987); Cecilia Elizabeth O'Leary, " 'Blood Brotherhood': The Racialization of Patriotism, 1865–1918," in *Bonds of Affection: Americans Define Their Patriotism,* ed. John Bodnar (Princeton: Princeton University Press, 1997), 53–81; John Pettegrew, "The Soldier's Faith: Turn-of-the-Century Memory of the Civil War and the Emergence of Modern American Nationalism," *Journal of Contemporary History* 31 (1996): 49–73; and Savage, *Standing Soldiers, Kneeling Slaves.*

18. Alice Fahs describes the widespread demands for realist Civil War literature that could provide realistic accounts of battle experiences. She credits Steven Crane's 1895 book *Red Badge of Courage* for inspiring this movement. Young in particular criticizes the realist turn in Civil War literature and links it to an increasingly masculine memory of the war. See Fahs, "The Feminized Civil War," 1488.

19. John Bodnar, *Remaking America: Public Memory, Commemoration, and Patriotism in the Twentieth Century* (Princeton: Princeton University Press, 1992), 12.

20. James E. Young, *The Texture of Memory: Holocaust Memorials and Meaning* (New Haven: Yale University Press, 1993) 12.

21. Michael S. Sherry, *In the Shadow of War: The United States since the 1930s* (New Haven: Yale University Press, 1995), x.

22. Michael Kammen, *Mystic Chords of Memory: The Transformation of Tradition in American Culture* (New York: Knopf, 1992), 13.

23. Rhetorical scholars with an interest in public memories of war have attended closely in recent years to the surge of World War II commemoration. See Barbara A. Biesecker, "Remembering World War II: The Rhetoric and Politics of National Commemoration at the Turn of the 21st Century," *Quarterly Journal of Speech* 88 (2002): 393–409; Peter Erenhaus, "Why We Fought: Holocaust Memory in Spielberg's *Saving Private Ryan,*" *Critical Studies in Media Communication* 18 (2001): 321–37; Marouf Hasian Jr., "Collective Amnesias: The Rudolph Kastner Trial and Holocaust Consciousness in Israel, 1948–1955," *Southern Communication Journal* 69 (2004): 136–56; and Susan A. Owen, "Memory, War and American Identity: *Saving Private Ryan* as Cinematic Jeremiad," *Critical Studies in Media Communication* 19 (2002): 249–82.

24. David W. Blight and Brooks S. Simpson, eds., *Union and Emancipation: Essays on Politics and Race in the Civil War Era* (Kent: Kent State University Press, 1997), 27.

25. See Barry Schwartz, "The Reconstruction of Abraham Lincoln," in *Collective Remembering,* ed. David Middleton and Derek Edwards (London: Sage Publications, 1990), 81–107.

26. Blight, "'For Something beyond the Battlefield,'" 1159.

27. Savage, *Standing Soldiers, Kneeling Slaves,* 3.

28. Ibid., 125–30.

29. See Thomas Connelly and Barbara L. Bellows, *God and General Longstreet: The Lost Cause and the Southern Mind* (Baton Rouge: Louisiana State University Press, 1982).

30. Ibid., 39–72.

31. G. Kurt Piehler, *Remembering War the American Way* (Washington, DC: Smithsonian Institution Press, 1995), 48–86; Savage, *Standing Soldiers, Kneeling Slaves,* 162–209.

32. Savage, *Standing Soldiers, Kneeling Slaves,* 210.

33. Quoted in Linenthal, *Sacred Ground,* 94.

34. Blight, "'For Something beyond the Battlefield,'" 1159.

35. Ibid., 1161.

36. Piehler, *Remembering War the American Way,* 49.

37. Ibid., 72.

38. Ibid.

39. Hal Rothman, *Preserving Different Pasts: The American National Monuments* (Urbana: University of Illinois Press, 1989), 34–52.

40. Bodnar, *Remaking America,* 170.

41. Harlan D. Unrau and G. Frank Williss, "To Preserve the Nation's Past: The Growth of Historic Preservation in the National Park Service during the 1930s," *Public Historian* 9 (1987): 19–50.

42. Everhart, *The National Park Service,* 5.

43. Rothman, *Preserving Different Pasts,* xiii.

44. Ibid., 200.

45. Quoted in Unrau and Williss, "To Preserve the Nation's Past," 37.

46. Rothman, *Preserving Different Pasts,* 201.

47. Ibid., 201.

48. Boge and Boge, *Paving Over the Past,* 5–8; Joan M. Zenzen, *Battling for Manassas: The Fifty-Year Preservation Struggle at Manassas National Battlefield Park* (University Park: Pennsylvania State University Press, 1998), xx–xxi.

49. Zenzen, *Battling for Manassas,* xxi.

50. For a comprehensive overview of NPS changes to its interpretive history programs in the 1990s and early 2000s, see Dwight Pitcaithley, "Taking the Long Way from Euterpe to Clio," in *Becoming Historians,* ed. James M. Banner and John R. Gillis (Chicago: University of Chicago Press, 2009), 55–76.

51. Quoted in Philip Kennicott, "At Last, a Gettysburg Redress; With Its New (but Old-Fashioned) Visitor Center and a Plan to Restore Sightlines, the Battlefield Honors Its Past," *Washington Post,* April 14, 2008, C1.

52. Hartwig, private conversation, February 8, 2007.

Chapter 1

1. 1. Four score and seven years ago our fathers brought forth on
    2. this continent, a new nation, conceived in liberty, and dedicated
    3. to the proposition that all men are created equal.
    4. Now we are engaged in a great civil war, testing whether that
    5. nation or any nation so conceived and so dedicated, can long
    6. endure. We are met on a great battle-field of that war. We have
    7. come to dedicate a portion of that field, as a final resting place
    8. for those who here gave their lives that that nation might live.
    9. It is altogether fitting and proper that we should do this.
    10. But in a larger sense, we can not dedicate—we can not
    11. consecrate—we can not hallow—this ground. The brave men, living
    12. and dead, who struggled here, have consecrated it, far above our
    13. poor power to add or detract. The world will little note, nor long
    14. remember what we say here, but it can never forget what they did
    15. here. It is for us the living, rather, to be dedicated here to the
    16. unfinished work which they who fought here have thus far so nobly
    17. advanced. It is rather for us to be here dedicated to the great
    18. task remaining before us—that from these honored dead we take
    19. increased devotion to that cause for which they gave the last full
    20. measure of devotion—that we here highly resolve that these dead
    21. shall not have died in vain—that this nation, under God, shall
    22. have a new birth of freedom—and that government of the people,
        by the people, for the people, shall not perish from the earth.

2. For a discussion of the appropriateness of using the Gettysburg Address to commemorate the terrorist attacks of September 11, 2001, see Joyce Purnick, "A Dissent on Hallowing 9/11 Ground," *New York Times,* September 5, 2002, B1. For a critique of seemingly transcendent and nonpartisan political speech used during New York's commemorative ceremonies on September 11, 2002, see Bradford Vivian, "Neoliberal Epideictic: Rhetorical Form and Commemorative Politics on September 12, 2002," *Quarterly Journal of Speech* 92, no. 1 (2006): 1–26.

3. Barry Schwartz provides a comprehensive analysis of the Gettysburg Address in public memory. See Schwartz, "Rereading the Gettysburg Address: Social Change and Collective Memory," *Qualitative Sociology* 19 (1996): 395–422.

4. See Gilbert Highet, "The Gettysburg Address," in *Readings in Speech,* ed. Haig A. Bosmajian, 2nd ed. (New York: Harper and Row, 1971), 221–27; and Earl W. Wiley, "Abraham Lincoln: His Emergence as the Voice of the People," in *A History and Criticism of American Public Address,* ed. William Norwood Brigance (New York: McGraw Hill, 1943), 2:869–71.

5. The most thorough rhetorical critique of the speech is by Edwin Black. See Black, "Gettysburg and Silence," *Quarterly Journal of Speech* 80 (February 1994): 21–

36. For a Burkean analysis of the Gettysburg Address, see Thomas F. Mader, "Burkean Rites and the Gettysburg Address," in *Rhetorical Movement: Essays in Honor of Leland M. Griffin,* ed. David Zarefsky (Evanston, IL: Northwestern University Press, 1993), 131–54. Harold Zyskind analyzes the speech's "hourglass" shape in "A Rhetorical Analysis of the Gettysburg Address," *Journal of General Education* 4 (1950): 202–12.

6. Several scholarly essays have called for an increased interest in how rhetors, audiences, and rhetorical critics facilitate multiple interpretations of seminal oral texts. For an excellent review and synthesis of these essays, see Leah Ceccarelli, "Polysemy: Multiple Meanings in Rhetorical Criticism," *Quarterly Journal of Speech* 84 (1998): 395–415.

7. Edward Linenthal refers to this public memory of the war as an "ideology of reconciliation." See Linenthal, *Sacred Ground,* 89–126. David W. Blight provides what is probably the most comprehensive history of "reconciliationist memory." See Blight, *Race and Reunion: The Civil War in American Memory* (Cambridge, MA: Harvard University Press, 2001).

8. Kirk Savage argues that the "common soldier" monument exploded across rural America in the late nineteenth and early twentieth centuries. Very little distinguished the Union soldier from the Confederate, which helped the country, Savage argues, create a composite common war hero that blurred regional differences between the two warring sides. Savage, *Standing Soldiers, Kneeling Slaves.*

9. I borrow the term "Savior of the Union" from Merrill D. Peterson's taxonomy of Lincoln personages in collective memory. See Peterson, *Lincoln in American Memory* (New York: Oxford University Press, 1994), 7–11.

10. Blight outlines the characteristics of emancipationist memory in *Race and Reunion,* 10–24.

11. Other scholars have analyzed Gettysburg as sacred place. For an analysis of how various groups have come to the battlefield to challenge the official ideology created in the Park Service space, see Linenthal, *Sacred Ground;* for a cultural history of Gettysburg, see Amy J. Kinsel, "'From These Honored Dead': Gettysburg in American Culture, 1863–1938" (Ph.D. diss., Cornell University, 1992); for a geographical history of the Gettysburg battlefield and cemetery, see Benjamin Yarber Dixon, "Gettysburg: A Living Battlefield" (Ph.D. diss., University of Oklahoma, 2000); for a rhetorical analysis of Franklin Delano Roosevelt's commemorative addresses at Gettysburg in 1934 and 1938, see Benson, "FDR at Gettysburg."

12. Black, "Gettysburg and Silence."

13. Gary W. Gallagher and Alan T. Nolan, eds., *The Myth of the Lost Cause and Civil War History* (Bloomington: Indiana University Press, 2000), 12.

14. Garry Wills, *Lincoln at Gettysburg: The Words That Remade America* (New York: Simon and Schuster, 1992), 41–62.

15. Black, "Gettysburg and Silence," 25.

16. The photograph was incorrectly marked, it turns out. Reynolds was killed in McPherson's Woods northwest of town. For an analysis of the historical context

of this photo, see William A. Frassanito, *Gettysburg: A Journey in Time* (New York: Charles Scribner's Sons, 1975), 224–28.

17. Quoted in Kinsel, "'From These Honored Dead,'" 94.

18. Halbwachs, *On Collective Memory*, 78.

19. Ibid.

20. Barry Schwartz, "Collective Memory and History: How Abraham Lincoln Became a Symbol of Racial Equality," *Sociological Quarterly* 38, no. 3 (1994): 470.

21. Ibid., 471.

22. National Park Service, *Gettysburg: Official Map and Guide* (Washington, DC: U.S. Department of the Interior, 1999).

23. Harlan D. Unrau, *Administrative History: Gettysburg National Military Park and National Cemetery* (Washington, DC: U.S. Department of the Interior, 1991), 325–27.

24. Carol Reardon, *Pickett's Charge in History and Memory* (Chapel Hill: University of North Carolina Press, 1997), 54–55.

25. Dixon, "Gettysburg: A Living Battlefield," 246.

26. Reardon, *Pickett's Charge in History and Memory*, 1–10.

27. Gallagher and Nolan, *The Myth of the Lost Cause and Civil War History*, 4.

28. Ibid., 12.

29. Dixon, "Gettysburg: A Living Battlefield," 240–78.

30. Richard Morris, *Sinners, Lovers, and Heroes: An Essay on Memorializing in Three American Cultures* (Albany: State University of New York Press, 1997), 77–152.

31. Quoted in ibid., 105.

32. Ibid., 115–52.

33. Ibid., 141.

34. Peter Novick, *That Noble Dream: The "Objectivity Question" and the American Historical Profession* (Cambridge: Cambridge University Press, 1988), 72–80.

35. A number of journalists provided thorough reviews of the new Museum and Visitor Center. See, for example, Dave Caldwell, "At Gettysburg, Farther from the Battle but Closer to History," *New York Times*, March 12, 2008, H30; Jayne Clark, "Battle of Gettysburg Hits Home in New $103 Million Museum: Theaters, Galleries Bring Huge Site into Better Focus," *USA Today*, April 11, 2008, 5D; Robert N. Jenkins, "Gettysburg Revisited," *St. Petersburg Times*, June 29, 2008, 4L; and Kennicott, "At Last, a Gettysburg Redress."

36. Quoted in Amy Worden, "Reinforcing History," *Philadelphia Inquirer*, April 13, 2008, B1.

37. The gallery housing Philippoteaux's renovated mural opened in September 2008.

38. The nonprofit Gettysburg Foundation raised funds for the new visitor center and will oversee its operations.

39. Quoted in Chris Satullo, "New Center at Gettysburg Links Old Issues to Today," *Philadelphia Inquirer*, September 20, 2008, B1.

40. Barry Schwartz provides a comprehensive analysis of the Gettysburg Address in public memory. See Schwartz, "Rereading the Gettysburg Address."

41. Editorial, *Gettysburg Times,* November 19, 1963, 6.

42. See Linenthal, *Sacred Ground,* 97–103.

43. Schwartz, "Rereading the Gettysburg Address," 414.

44. John Hennessy, chief historian at Fredericksburg and Spotsylvania National Military Park, discussed the agency's reactive role in a private telephone conversation with the author on August 10, 2009.

Chapter 2

1. See, for example, Blight, *Race and Reunion;* Blight, " 'For Something beyond the Battlefield' "; Fahs, "The Feminized Civil War"; Foster, *Ghosts of the Confederacy;* O'Leary, " 'Blood Brotherhood' "; Pettegrew, "The Soldier's Faith"; and Savage, *Standing Soldiers, Kneeling Slaves.*

2. Nina Silber, *Romance of Reunion: Northerners and the South, 1865–1890* (Chapel Hill: University of North Carolina Press, 1993).

3. For a detailed account of Brown's raid, including Shepherd's shooting, see Stephen B. Oates, *To Purge This Land of Blood: A Biography of John Brown* (Amherst: University of Massachusetts Press, 1984), 274–306.

4. Three outstanding accounts of Southern Lost Cause memory of the Civil War are Connelly and Bellows, *God and General Longstreet;* Foster, *Ghosts of the Confederacy;* and Gallagher and Nolan, *The Myth of the Lost Cause and Civil War History.*

5. The only other artifact of memory located inside the park and not created by the Park Service is a monument to John Brown dedicated in 1918 by Storer College alumni. Located in Harpers Ferry, Storer College was one of the first schools of higher learning open to blacks following the Civil War. I discuss the monument on pages 66–67.

6. Paul A. Shackel provides an excellent overview of the Heyward Shepherd Memorial as an example of the "faithful-slave" monument. See Shackel, *Memory in Black and White: Race, Commemoration, and the Post-Bellum Landscape* (New York: Rowman and Littlefield, 2003), 77–112.

7. For a discussion of history and myth as distinct genres of forms of memory, see John Michael Janas, "Rhetoric, History, and the Collective Memory: The Civil War in Contemporary America" (Ph.D. diss., University of Iowa, 1994).

8. The term "emancipationist memory" was coined by Blight, *Race and Reunion,* 2–5.

9. Park interpretation completed in the 1990s includes the John Brown Museum, Civil War Museum, African-American History Museum, and the refurbished Visitors Center.

10. Park Service administrators typically define preservation as preceding and delimiting the second objective of interpretation. For example, former NPS assistant director of historic preservation Robert Utley argues that the Park Service's objectives were twofold: "First, we were to care for 'historic resources' and guard them from whatever forces, natural or human (including our own managers), endangered

them. The historic resources of battlefields are the terrain, vegetative cover, road systems, buildings, and other structures that have survived from the time of the battle. Second, we were to 'interpret' these resources through museums, films, publications, lectures, tours, and other media, to give the visitor an understanding and appreciation of the resources and the events being illustrated." Quoted in Linenthal, *Sacred Ground,* ix–x.

11. Merritt Roe Smith, *Harpers Ferry Armory and the New Technology* (Ithaca, NY: Cornell University Press, 1977).

12. Bertram Wyatt-Brown, " 'A Volcano beneath a Mountain of Snow': John Brown and the Problem of Interpretation," in *His Soul Goes Marching On: Responses to John Brown and the Harpers Ferry Raid,* ed. Paul Finkelman (Charlottesville: University Press of Virginia, 1995), 10–38.

13. Paul Finkelman, "Manufacturing Martyrdom: The Antislavery Response to John Brown's Raid," in *His Soul Goes Marching On: Responses to John Brown and the Harpers Ferry Raid,* ed. Paul Finkelman (Charlottesville: University Press of Virginia, 1995), 41–66.

14. Daniel C. Littlefield wrote an excellent article describing the subtle differences between black and white antislavery responses to Brown's raid. See Littlefield, "Blacks, John Brown, and a Theory of Manhood," in *His Soul Goes Marching On: Responses to John Brown and the Harpers Ferry Raid,* ed. Paul Finkelman (Charlottesville: University Press of Virginia, 1995), 70–88.

15. Marouf Hasian Jr., "Jurisprudence as Performance: John Brown's Enactment of Natural Law at Harper's Ferry," *Quarterly Journal of Speech* 86, no. 2 (2000): 190–214.

16. Ibid., 207–9.

17. Ibid., 209.

18. Quoted in Oates, *To Purge This Land of Blood,* 305.

19. Quoted in Hasian, "Jurisprudence as Performance," 204.

20. Robert E. Mcglone explores the politics of defining Brown's insanity during his trial in "John Brown, Henry Wise, and the Politics of Insanity," in *His Soul Goes Marching On: Responses to John Brown and the Harpers Ferry Raid,* ed. Paul Finkelman (Charlottesville: University Press of Virginia, 1995), 213–52.

21. Quoted in ibid., 222.

22. Allan Nevins, *The Statesmanship of the Civil War* (New York: Macmillan, 1953), 29–30.

23. Peter Novick observes that American historians' overwhelming support of history as an objective science led many to create "balanced" histories of the war that privileged neither a Southern nor a Northern interpretation of the war. This compromise, in an effort to avoid a "partisan" history of the war, nevertheless re-created the "reconciliationist" memory of the war that did exclude other social groups' memories of the war, especially those of blacks. Novick, *That Noble Dream,* 234–39.

24. Close textual analysis of museum exhibits, which is privileged in this study,

restricts the number of museums that can be analyzed in each park. The John Brown Museum, because of its centrality to the park and the Park Service's overall narrative of Harpers Ferry, is given extended attention in this study. The museum is also representative of the recent exhibits that interpret the past from an emancipationist perspective.

25. Linenthal, *Sacred Ground,* xi.

26. The most concrete evidence for reunification cited by Blight are the congressional election results of 1874 and the compromises made between northern Republicans and southern Democrats to satisfy the dispute over the presidential election of Rutherford B. Hayes in 1876. Both Hayes and Samuel J. Tilden, the Democratic candidate for president, were moderate reconciliationists. See Blight, *Race and Reunion,* 130–39.

27. Blight, *Race and Reunion,* 300–380.

28. Blight identifies Washington's rhetoric as reconciliationist. See *Race and Reunion,* 324–37.

29. Quoted in Blight, *Race and Reunion,* 320.

30. For a discussion of nineteenth-century black millennial thought, see Blight, *Race and Reunion,* 320–24.

31. Recent debates in South Carolina and Mississippi over the right to fly the Confederate flag on state capitol grounds are one example of an active rhetorical battleground of Civil War memory. For a discussion of Confederate flag debates, see Janas, "Rhetoric, History, and the Collective Memory," 137–91. "Preservation" versus "economic growth" debates such as the one involving Disney's proposed history-based theme park near Manassas National Battlefield Park in the early 1990s is another example of Civil War memory playing an explicit role in public debates. For examples of these debates, see Boge and Boge, *Paving Over the Past,* and Kennedy, *Dollar$ and Sense of Battlefield Preservation.*

Chapter 3

1. Carol Reardon argues that the historical truth of the final Confederate charge of the Union center line on the battle's decisive third day gradually became overshadowed by the voices of memory. See Reardon, *Pickett's Charge in History and Memory.*

2. Historians such as Gary W. Gallagher are quick to note that in the late summer of 1863 few people believed that the Union victory at Gettysburg was decisive enough to put a sudden end to the war. Southerners' optimism, he argues, extended even into the spring of 1864. See Gallagher, *The Confederate War: How Popular Will, Nationalism, and Military Strategy Could Not Stave Off Defeat* (Cambridge, MA: Harvard University Press, 1997), 3–13.

3. Gerald F. Linderman, *Embattled Courage: The Experience of Combat in the American Civil War* (Urbana: University of Illinois Press, 1991), 17. Other notable books that examine and critique the Civil War as destructive include Michael Fellman,

Lesley Gordon, and Daniel Sutherland, *This Terrible War: The Civil War and Its Aftermath* (New York: Longman, 2003); Mark E. Neely Jr., *The Civil War and the Limits of Destruction* (Cambridge, MA: Harvard University Press, 2007); and Harry S. Stout, *Upon the Altar of the Nation: A Moral History of the Civil War* (New York: Penguin, 2006).

4. Linderman, *Embattled Courage,* 20.

5. Ibid., 21.

6. Quoted in ibid., 31.

7. Ibid., 10.

8. Ibid., 64.

9. Ibid., 125.

10. Ibid., 135.

11. Ibid.

12. Ibid., 145.

13. Sam Keen, *Faces of the Enemy: Images of the Hostile Imagination* (San Francisco: Harper and Row, 1986), 73.

14. Quoted in Linderman, *Embattled Courage,* 148–49.

15. Ibid., 153.

16. Ibid., 159.

17. Ibid., 206–7.

18. Much of my thoughts on this matter are informed by Elaine Scarry's examination of representations of torture and war. See Scarry, *The Body in Pain: The Making and Unmaking of the World* (New York: Oxford University Press, 1985), 63–91.

19. Scarry, *The Body in Pain,* 71.

20. See ibid., 67–68.

21. Ibid., 73.

22. Joanna Bourke, *An Intimate History of Killing: Face to Face Killing in 20th Century Warfare* (New York: Basic Books, 1999), xiii.

23. Quoted in Linderman, *Embattled Courage,* 148.

24. Ibid., 185.

Chapter 4

1. For an excellent analysis of the rhetoric of abstraction in war, see Keen, *Faces of the Enemy,* 73–86.

2. John Keegan, *The Face of Battle* (New York: Viking Press, 1976).

3. Timothy Sweet, *Traces of War: Poetry, Photography, and the Crisis of the Union* (Baltimore: Johns Hopkins University Press, 1990), 96.

4. Ibid., 99.

5. Blight, *Race and Reunion,* 222.

6. This might help explain NPS supporters' aggressive resistance to the encroachments of modernization on and around the Gettysburg battlefield, such as the re-

cently removed observation tower and the proliferation of tourist attractions located throughout the town of Gettysburg.

7. Quoted in Linenthal, *Sacred Ground,* 84.

8. Amy Kinsel describes the memorial's history in " 'From These Honored Dead,' " 270–74.

9. Savage, *Standing Soldiers, Kneeling Slaves.*

10. See Sweet, *Traces of War,* 107–37.

11. Alexander Gardner, *Gardner's Photographic Sketch Book of the Civil War* (New York: Dover Publications, 1959), ix.

12. Frassanito, *Gettysburg,* 182–83.

13. Ibid., 27.

Chapter 5

1. There are several excellent accounts of the fighting at Cold Harbor. See especially Ernest B. Furgurson, *Not War But Murder: Cold Harbor, 1864* (New York: Knopf, 2000), and Gordon C. Rhea, *Cold Harbor: Grant and Lee, May 26–June 3, 1864* (Baton Rouge: Louisiana State University Press, 2002).

2. Stout, *Upon the Altar of the Nation,* 348.

3. Quoted in Furgurson, *Not War But Murder,* 88.

4. For a fascinating examination of trench warfare during the Overland Campaign, see Earl J. Hess, *Trench Warfare under Grant and Lee: Field Fortifications in the Overland Campaign* (Chapel Hill: University of North Carolina Press, 2007).

5. Quoted in Stout, *Upon the Altar of the Nation,* 333.

6. Ibid., 343.

7. Quoted in Gordon C. Rhea, *The Battle of Cold Harbor* (National Park Service Civil War Series, Eastern National, 2001), 42.

8. Furgurson, *Not War But Murder,* 134.

9. Quoted in ibid.

10. Quoted in Rhea, *Battle of Cold Harbor,* 45–46.

11. For an administrative history of Richmond National Battlefield Park, see Joseph P. Cullen, *Richmond National Battlefield Park, Virginia,* vol. 33 (National Park Service Historical Handbook Series, 1961).

12. See Scarry, *The Body in Pain,* 63–91.

13. Timothy Sweet develops a nuanced analysis of the portrayal of nature in Civil War photography, which has informed my thinking about the Park Service's representation of its preserved natural spaces. See Sweet, *Traces of War.*

14. Quoted in Drew Gilpin Faust's remarkable book, *This Republic of Suffering: Death and the American Civil War* (New York: Knopf, 2008), 118. For another excellent description of soldiers' widespread derision toward sharpshooters, see Linderman, *Embattled Courage,* 148–49.

15. Quoted in Faust, *This Republic of Suffering,* 9.

16. Gardner, *Gardner's Photographic Sketch Book of the Civil War.*

17. For an analysis of Gardner's "Burial Party" photograph, see Alan Trachtenberg, "Albums of War: On Reading Civil War Photographs," *Representations* 9 (1985): 1–32.

18. Gardner's "Harvest of Death" photograph of soldiers killed at Gettysburg is particularly haunting. See Gardner, *Gardner's Photographic Sketch Book of the Civil War,* and Anthony W. Lee and Elizabeth Young's analysis of the photo in *On Alexander Gardner's "Photographic Sketch Book of the Civil War"* (Berkeley: University of California Press, 2007).

19. This oft-cited quote comes from Carl von Clausewitz's *On War* (New York: Barnes and Noble, 1968).

20. Quoted in Faust, *This Republic of Suffering,* xii.

Conclusion

1. Hennessy, private conversation, August 10, 2009.

2. Ibid.

Bibliography

Albright, Horace M., and Robert Cahn. *The Birth of the National Park Service: The Founding Years, 1913–33.* Salt Lake City: Howe Brothers, 1985.

Armada, Bernard J. "Memorial Agon: An Interpretive Tour of the National Civil Rights Museum." *Southern Communication Journal* 63 (1998): 235–43.

Bearss, Edwin C. "The National Park Service and Its History Program: 1866–1986—An Overview." *Public Historian* 9 (1987): 10–18.

Benson, Thomas W. "FDR at Gettysburg: The New Deal and the Rhetoric of Presidential Leadership." In *The Rhetoric of Presidential Leadership,* ed. Leroy Dorsey. College Station: Texas A&M University Press, 2002. 145–83.

Biesecker, Barbara A. "Remembering World War II: The Rhetoric and Politics of National Commemoration at the Turn of the 21st Century." *Quarterly Journal of Speech* 88 (2002): 393–409.

Black, Edwin. "Gettysburg and Silence." *Quarterly Journal of Speech* 80 (February 1994): 21–36.

Blair, Carole, Marsha S. Jeppeson, and Enrico Pucci Jr. "Public Memorializing in Postmodernity: The Vietnam Veterans Memorial as Prototype." *Quarterly Journal of Speech* 77 (1991): 263–88.

Blair, Carol, and Neil Michel. "Commemorating in the Theme Park Zone: Reading the Astronauts Memorial." In *At the Intersection: Cultural Studies and Rhetorical Studies,* ed. Thomas Rosteck. New York: Guilford, 1999. 29–83.

———. "Reproducing Civil Rights Tactics: The Rhetorical Performances of the Civil Rights Memorial." *Rhetoric Society Quarterly* 30 (1999): 31–55.

Blight, David W. " 'For Something beyond the Battlefield': Frederick Douglass and the Struggle for the Memory of the Civil War." *Journal of American History* (1989): 1156–78.

———. *Race and Reunion: The Civil War in American Memory.* Cambridge, MA: Harvard University Press, 2001.

Blight, David W., and Brooks S. Simpson, eds. *Union and Emancipation: Essays on Politics and Race in the Civil War Era.* Kent: Kent State University Press, 1997.

Bodnar, John. *Remaking America: Public Memory, Commemoration, and Patriotism in the Twentieth Century.* Princeton: Princeton University Press, 1992.

Boge, Georgie, and Margie Holder Boge. *Paving Over the Past: A History and Guide to Civil War Battlefield Preservation.* Washington, DC: Island Press, 1993.

Bourke, Joanna. *An Intimate History of Killing: Face to Face Killing in 20th Century Warfare.* New York: Basic Books, 1999.

Bowman, Michael S. "Looking for Stonewall's Arm: Tourist Performance as Research Method." In *Opening Acts: Performance in/as Communication and Cultural Studies,* ed. Judith Hamera. Thousand Oaks, CA: Sage, 2005. 102–33.

Browne, Stephen H. "Reading Public Memory in Daniel Webster's Plymouth Rock Oration." *Western Journal of Communication* 57 (1993): 464–77.

———. "Reading, Rhetoric, and the Texture of Public Memory." *Quarterly Journal of Speech* 81 (1995): 257–65.

Burke, Kenneth. *A Grammar of Motives.* Berkeley: University of California Press, 1969.

Caldwell, Dave. "At Gettysburg, Farther from the Battle but Closer to History." *New York Times,* March 12, 2008, H30.

Carlson, A. Cheree, and John E. Hocking. "Strategies of Redemption at the Vietnam Veterans' Memorial." *Western Journal of Speech Communication* 52 (1988): 203–15.

Ceccarelli, Leah. "Polysemy: Multiple Meanings in Rhetorical Criticism." *Quarterly Journal of Speech* 84 (1998): 395–415.

Clark, Jayne. "Battle of Gettysburg Hits Home in New $103 Million Museum: Theaters, Galleries Bring Huge Site into Better Focus." *USA Today,* April 11, 2008, 5D.

Clausewitz, Carl V. *On War.* New York: Barnes and Noble, 1968.

Connelly, Thomas, and Barbara L. Bellows. *God and General Longstreet: The Lost Cause and the Southern Mind.* Baton Rouge: Louisiana State University Press, 1982.

Connerton, Paul. *How Societies Remember.* Cambridge: Cambridge University Press, 1989.

Davies, Wallace Evan. *Patriotism on Parade: The Story of Veterans' and Hereditary Organizations in America, 1783–1900.* Cambridge, MA: Harvard University Press, 1955.

DeLuca, Kevin Michael, and Anne Teresa Demo. "Imaging Nature: Yosemite and the Birth of Environmentalism." *Critical Studies in Media Communication* 17 (2000): 241–60.

Desjardin, Thomas A. *These Honored Dead: How the Story of Gettysburg Shaped American Memory.* Cambridge, MA: Da Capo Press, 2003.

Dixon, Benjamin Yarber. "Gettysburg: A Living Battlefield." Ph.D. diss., University of Oklahoma, 2000.

Edsall, Thomas, and Mary Edsall. *Chain Reaction: The Impact of Race, Rights and Taxes on American Politics.* New York: Norton, 1991.

Erenhaus, Peter. "Why We Fought: Holocaust Memory in Spielberg's *Saving Private Ryan.*" *Critical Studies in Media Communication* 18 (2001): 321–37.

Evans, Martin. *War and Memory in the Twentieth Century.* New York: Oxford University Press, 1997.

Everhart, William C. *The National Park Service.* Boulder, CO: Westview Press, 1983.

Fahs, Alice. "The Feminized Civil War: Gender, Northern Popular Literature, and the Memory of the War, 1861–1900." *Journal of American History* (1999): 1461–94.

Faust, Drew Gilpin. *The Creation of Confederate Nationalism: Ideology and Identity in the Civil War South.* Baton Rouge: Louisiana State University Press, 1988.

———. *This Republic of Suffering: Death and the American Civil War.* New York: Knopf, 2008.

Fellman, Michael, Lesley Gordon, and Daniel Sutherland. *This Terrible War: The Civil War and Its Aftermath.* New York: Longman, 2003.

Finkelman, Paul. "Manufacturing Martyrdom: The Antislavery Response to John Brown's Raid." In *His Soul Goes Marching On: Responses to John Brown and the Harpers Ferry Raid,* ed. Paul Finkelman. Charlottesville: University Press of Virginia, 1995. 41–66.

Fisher, Walter. *Human Communication as Narration: Toward a Philosophy of Reason, Value, and Action.* Columbia: University of South Carolina Press, 1987.

Foote, Kenneth E. *Shadowed Ground: America's Landscapes of Violence and Tragedy.* Austin: University of Texas Press, 1997.

Foster, Gaines M. *Ghosts of the Confederacy: Defeat, the Lost Cause, and the Emergence of the New South.* New York: Oxford University Press, 1987.

Frassanito, William A. *Gettysburg: A Journey in Time.* New York: Charles Scribner's Sons, 1975.

Furgurson, Ernest B. *Not War But Murder: Cold Harbor, 1864.* New York: Knopf, 2000.

Fussell, Paul. *The Great War and Modern Memory.* New York: Oxford University Press, 1975.

Gallagher, Gary W. *Causes Won, Lost, and Forgotten: How Hollywood and Popular Art Shape What We Know about the Civil War.* Chapel Hill: University of North Carolina Press, 2008.

———. *The Confederate War: How Popular Will, Nationalism, and Military Strategy Could Not Stave Off Defeat.* Cambridge, MA: Harvard University Press, 1997.

Gallagher, Gary W., and Alan T. Nolan, eds. *The Myth of the Lost Cause and Civil War History.* Bloomington: Indiana University Press, 2000.

Gallagher, Victoria J. "Memory and Reconciliation in the Birmingham Civil Rights Institute." *Rhetoric and Public Affairs* 2 (1999): 303–20.

———. "Remembering Together: Rhetorical Integration and the Case of the Martin Luther King, Jr. Memorial." *Southern Communication Journal* 60 (1995): 109–19.

Gardner, Alexander. *Gardner's Photographic Sketch Book of the Civil War.* New York: Dover Publications, 1959.

Gillis, John R. "Memory and Identity: The History of a Relationship." In *Commemorations: The Politics of National Identity,* ed. John R. Gillis. Princeton: Princeton University Press, 1994. 3–24.

Halbwachs, Maurice. *On Collective Memory.* Trans. Lewis A. Coser. Chicago: University of Chicago Press, 1992. Trans. of *Les cadres sociaux de la mémoire.* Paris: Presses Universitaires de France, 1952.

Hasian, Marouf, Jr. "Collective Amnesias: The Rudolph Kastner Trial and Holocaust Consciousness in Israel, 1948–1955." *Southern Communication Journal* 69 (2004): 136–56.

———. "Jurisprudence as Performance: John Brown's Enactment of Natural Law at Harpers Ferry." *Quarterly Journal of Speech* 86, no. 2 (2000): 190–214.

Hess, Earl J. *Trench Warfare under Grant and Lee: Field Fortifications in the Overland Campaign.* Chapel Hill: University of North Carolina Press, 2007.

Highet, Gilbert. "The Gettysburg Address." In *Readings in Speech,* ed. Haig A. Bosmajian. 2nd ed. New York: Harper and Row, 1971. 221–27.

Janas, John Michael. "Rhetoric, History, and the Collective Memory: The Civil War in Contemporary America." Ph.D. diss., University of Iowa, 1994.

Jenkins, Robert N. "Gettysburg Revisited." *St. Petersburg Times,* June 29, 2008, 4L.

Jorgensen-Earp, Cheryl R., and Lori A. Lanzilotti. "Public Memory and Private Grief: The Construction of Shrines at the Sites of Public Tragedy." *Quarterly Journal of Speech* 84 (1998): 150–70.

Kammen, Michael. *Mystic Chords of Memory: The Transformation of Tradition in American Culture.* New York: Knopf, 1992.

Katriel, Tamar. *Performing the Past: A Study of Israeli Settlement Museums.* Mahwah, NJ: Lawrence Erlbaum, 1997.

Keegan, John. *The Face of Battle.* New York: Viking Press, 1976.

Keen, Sam. *Faces of the Enemy: Images of the Hostile Imagination.* San Francisco: Harper and Row, 1986.

Kennedy, Frances H. *Dollar$ and Sense of Battlefield Preservation: The Economic Benefits of Protecting Civil War Battlefields.* Washington, DC: Preservation Press, 1994.

Kennicott, Philip. "At Last, a Gettysburg Redress; With Its New (but Old-Fashioned) Visitor Center and a Plan to Restore Sightlines, the Battlefield Honors Its Past." *Washington Post,* April 14, 2008, C1.

Kinsel, Amy J. "'From These Honored Dead': Gettysburg in American Culture, 1863–1938." Ph.D. diss., Cornell University, 1992.

Lee, Anthony W., and Elizabeth Young. *On Alexander Gardner's "Photographic Sketch Book of the Civil War."* Berkeley: University of California Press, 2007.

Linderman, Gerald F. *Embattled Courage: The Experience of Combat in the American Civil War.* Urbana: University of Illinois Press, 1991.

Linenthal, Edward T. *Sacred Ground: Americans and Their Battlefields.* Urbana: University of Illinois Press, 1991.

Littlefield, Daniel C. "Blacks, John Brown, and a Theory of Manhood." In *His Soul Goes Marching On: Responses to John Brown and the Harpers Ferry Raid,* ed. Paul Finkelman. Charlottesville: University Press of Virginia, 1995.

Loewen, James W. *Lies across America: What Our Historic Sites Get Wrong.* New York: New Press, 1999.

Lowenthal, David. *The Past Is a Foreign Country.* Cambridge: Cambridge University Press, 1985.

Mackintosh, Barry. "The National Park Service Moves into Historical Interpretation." *Public Historian* 9 (1987): 51–64.

Mader, Thomas F. "Burkean Rites and the Gettysburg Address." In *Rhetorical Movement: Essays in Honor of Leland M. Griffin,* ed. David Zarefsky. Evanston, IL: Northwestern University Press, 1993. 131–54.

Mayo, James. *War Memorials as Political Landscape: The American Experience and Beyond.* New York: Praeger, 1988.

Mcglone, Robert E. "John Brown, Henry Wise, and the Politics of Insanity." In *His Soul Goes Marching On: Responses to John Brown and the Harpers Ferry Raid,* ed. Paul Finkelman. Charlottesville: University Press of Virginia. 213–52.

Miller, Page Putnam. "Reflections on Historical Advocacy and the National Park Service." *Public Historian* 9 (1987): 105–13.

Morris, Richard. *Sinners, Lovers, and Heroes: An Essay on Memorializing in Three American Cultures.* Albany: State University of New York Press, 1997.

Neely, Mark E., Jr. *The Civil War and the Limits of Destruction.* Cambridge, MA: Harvard University Press, 2007.

Nevins, Allan. *The Statesmanship of the Civil War.* New York: Macmillan, 1953.

Novick, Peter. *That Noble Dream: The "Objectivity Question" and the American Historical Profession.* Cambridge: Cambridge University Press, 1988.

Oates, Stephen B. *To Purge This Land of Blood: A Biography of John Brown.* Amherst: University of Massachusetts Press, 1984.

O'Leary, Cecilia Elizabeth. " 'Blood Brotherhood': The Racialization of Patriotism, 1865–1918." In *Bonds of Affection: Americans Define Their Patriotism,* ed. John Bodnar. Princeton: Princeton University Press, 1997. 53–81.

Owen, Susan A. "Memory, War and American Identity: *Saving Private Ryan* as Cinematic Jeremiad." *Critical Studies in Media Communication* 19 (2002): 249–82.

Patterson, John S. "From Battle Ground to Pleasure Ground: Gettysburg as a Historic Site." In *History Museums in the United States: A Critical Assessment,* ed. Warren Leon and Roy Rosenweig. Urbana: University of Illinois Press, 1989. 128–40.

Peterson, Merrill D. *Lincoln in American Memory.* New York: Oxford University Press, 1994.

Pettegrew, John. "The Soldier's Faith: Turn-of-the-Century Memory of the Civil War and the Emergence of Modern American Nationalism." *Journal of Contemporary History* 31 (1996): 49–73.

Phillips, Kendall R., ed. *Framing Public Memory.* Tuscaloosa: University of Alabama Press, 2004.

Piehler, G. Kurt. *Remembering War the American Way.* Washington, DC: Smithsonian Institution Press, 1995.

Pitcaithley, Dwight. " 'A Cosmic Threat': The National Park Service Addresses the Causes of the American Civil War." In *Slavery and Public History,* ed. James O. Horton and Lois E. Horton. New York: New Press, 2006.

———. "Taking the Long Way from Euterpe to Clio." In *Becoming Historians,* ed.

James M. Banner and John R. Gillis. Chicago: University of Chicago Press, 2009. 55–76.

Purnick, Joyce. "A Dissent on Hallowing 9/11 Ground." *New York Times,* September 5, 2002, B1.

Reardon, Carol. *Pickett's Charge in History and Memory.* Chapel Hill: University of North Carolina Press, 1997.

Rhea, Gordon C. *The Battle of Cold Harbor.* National Park Service Civil War Series, Eastern National, 2001.

———. *Cold Harbor: Grant and Lee, May 26–June 3, 1864.* Baton Rouge: Louisiana State University Press, 2002.

Rothman, Hal. *Preserving Different Pasts: The American National Monuments.* Urbana: University of Illinois Press, 1989.

Royster, Charles. *The Destructive War: William Tecumseh, Sherman, Stonewall Jackson, and the Americans.* New York: Vintage Books, 1991.

Runte, Alfred. *National Parks: The American Experience.* Lincoln: University of Nebraska Press, 1987.

Sandage, Scott. "A Marble House Divided: The Lincoln Memorial, the Civil Rights Movement, and the Politics of Memory, 1939–1963." *Journal of American History* 80 (June 1993): 135–67.

Satullo, Chris. "New Center at Gettysburg Links Old Issues to Today." *Philadelphia Inquirer,* September 20, 2008, B1.

Savage, Kirk. "The Politics of Memory: Black Emancipation and the Civil War Monument." In *Commemorations: The Politics of National Identity,* ed. John R. Gillis. Princeton: Princeton University Press, 1994. 128–49.

———. "Race, Memory, and Identity: The National Monuments of the Union and the Confederacy." Ph.D. diss., University of California, Berkeley, 1990.

———. *Standing Soldiers, Kneeling Slaves: Race, War, and Monument in Nineteenth-Century America.* Princeton: Princeton University Press, 1997.

Scarry, Elaine. *The Body in Pain: The Making and Unmaking of the World.* New York: Oxford University Press, 1985.

Schwartz, Barry. *Abraham Lincoln and the Forge of National Memory.* Chicago: University of Chicago Press, 2000.

———. "Collective Memory and History: How Abraham Lincoln Became a Symbol of Racial Equality." *Sociological Quarterly* 38, no. 3 (1994): 469–96.

———. "Postmodernity and Historical Reputation: Abraham Lincoln in Late Twentieth-Century American Memory." *Social Forces* 77 (September 1998): 63–103.

———. "The Reconstruction of Abraham Lincoln." In *Collective Remembering,* ed. David Middleton and Derek Edwards. London: Sage Publications, 1990. 81–107.

———. "Rereading the Gettysburg Address: Social Change and Collective Memory." *Qualitative Sociology* 19 (1996): 395–422.

Shackel, Paul A. *Memory in Black and White: Race, Commemoration, and the Post-Bellum Landscape.* New York: Rowman and Littlefield, 2003.

Sherry, Michael S. *In the Shadow of War: The United States since the 1930s*. New Haven: Yale University Press, 1995.

Silber, Nina. *Romance of Reunion: Northerners and the South, 1865–1890*. Chapel Hill: University of North Carolina Press, 1993.

Smith, Merritt Roe. *Harpers Ferry Armory and the New Technology*. Ithaca, NY: Cornell University Press, 1977.

Stout, Harry S. *Upon the Altar of the Nation: A Moral History of the Civil War*. New York: Viking, 2006.

Sutton, Robert K., ed. *Rally on the High Ground: The National Park Service Symposium on the Civil War, Ford's Theatre, May 8 and 9, 2000*. National Park Service, Eastern National, 2001.

Sweet, Timothy. *Traces of War: Poetry, Photography, and the Crisis of the Union*. Baltimore: Johns Hopkins University Press, 2001.

Thelen, David. "Memory and American History." *Journal of American History* 45 (1989): 1117–29.

Tilden, Freeman. *Interpreting Our Heritage*. Chapel Hill: University of North Carolina Press, 1977.

Trachtenberg, Alan. "Albums of War: On Reading Civil War Photographs." *Representations* 9 (1985): 1–32.

Unrau, Harlan D. *Administrative History: Gettysburg National Military Park and National Cemetery*. Washington, DC: U.S. Department of the Interior, 1991.

Unrau, Harlan D., and G. Frank Williss. "To Preserve the Nation's Past: The Growth of Historic Preservation in the National Park Service during the 1930s." *Public Historian* 9 (1987): 19–50.

Vivian, Bradford. "Neoliberal Epideictic: Rhetorical Form and Commemorative Politics on September 11, 2002." *Quarterly Journal of Speech* 92, no. 1 (2006): 1–26.

Warren, Leon, and Roy Rosenzweig. *History Museums in the United States: A Critical Assessment*. Urbana: University of Illinois Press, 1989.

Weaver, Bruce. "What to Do with the Mountain People? The Darker Side of the Successful Campaign to Establish the Great Smoky Mountains National Park." In *The Symbolic Earth: Discourse and Our Creation of the Environment*, ed. James G. Cantrill and Christine L. Oravec. Lexington: University of Kentucky Press, 1996.

Weeks, Jim. *Gettysburg: Memory, Market, and an American Shrine*. Princeton: Princeton University Press, 2003.

Wiley, Earl W. "Abraham Lincoln: His Emergence as the Voice of the People." In *A History and Criticism of American Public Address*, ed. William Norwood Brigance. New York: McGraw Hill, 1943. 2:869–71.

Wills, Garry. *Lincoln at Gettysburg: The Words That Remade America*. New York: Simon and Schuster, 1992.

Wirth, Conrad L. *Parks, Politics, and the People*. Norman: University of Oklahoma Press, 1980.

Worden, Amy. "Reinforcing History." *Philadelphia Inquirer*, April 13, 2008, B1.

Wright, Elizabethada A. "Rhetorical Spaces in Memorial Places: The Cemetery as a Rhetorical Memory Place/Space." *Rhetoric Society Quarterly* 35 (2005): 51–81.

Wyatt-Brown, Bertram. "'A Volcano beneath a Mountain of Snow': John Brown and the Problem of Interpretation." In *His Soul Goes Marching On: Responses to John Brown and the Harpers Ferry Raid,* ed. Paul Finkelman. Charlottesville: University Press of Virginia, 1995. 10–38.

Young, James E. *The Texture of Memory: Holocaust Memorials and Meaning.* New Haven: Yale University Press, 1993.

Zenzen, Joan M. *Battling for Manassas: The Fifty-Year Preservation Struggle at Manassas National Battlefield Park.* University Park: Pennsylvania State University Press, 1998.

Zyskind, Harold. "A Rhetorical Analysis of the Gettysburg Address." *Journal of General Education* 4 (1950): 202–12.

Index